by philippa hanna

More
Published by
Resound Media
Devonshire House
Eldon Street
Sheffield
S1 4NR

Resound Media represents a number of artists, writers and performers.
www.resoundmedia.co.uk
info@resoundmedia.co.uk

Printed by Book Printing UK

Artwork by Kate Tophill

In loving memory of Dell Cook...a modern-day saint.

Contents

Before Christ

dreams, teens, and tantrums

One of my earliest memories is being two years old and staring upwards at my dad. *My* dad. He's about to go on stage and belong to the audience but I've got his undivided attention for just a few minutes. He smells of Old Spice after-shave and when I hug him I can just about reach the silky panels at the back of his waistcoat. The one consolation in losing him to the audience is in the music. I love the music. At the back of the stage I colour in pictures and listen, stopping now and then to dance and pretend I'm out there with him.

Another early memory that sticks in my mind is the first time I recall *really* singing. I'm standing in the living room, my sister and my mum breaking off from their conversation to listen as I belt out a slightly exaggerated version of 'The Greatest Love of All'. They're beaming and asking me for another chorus. Dad comes in and they ask me to do it again, then dad's friend arrives and I sing it... again. I think I sang that song for every visitor we had over the next twelve months. I wasn't sure what the grown-ups liked about it. But when I opened my mouth, it seemed to come out nice and I never got tired of being asked.

All I ever wanted to do was sing in front of people. I got my first opportunity to take to the stage at the age of two. I begged and begged for my dad to let me be part of the talent show at the club in Skegness where he was the compere. Being on that stage was very different to how I'd imagined. It was so much bigger up there. The lights were so bright. All I could see was about a hundred pairs of legs through the mist of dry ice. The smell upset me. I just wanted to go back to the grabbing machines in the arcade. When the mirror ball sent a flurry of stars spinning around the room I'd had enough. I heard my voice begin to shout, "Turn those lights out! Turn those LIGHTS OUT!" The doting adults broke into fits of laughter. I was rather upset as dad came to rescue me. The stage team managed to find an old sports trophy in the cellar to make me feel better about the experience.

I was so eager to go out on that stage and sing. I knew all the words and thought I sounded just like Whitney. It felt so good to belt at the top of my voice, stretching out each note dramatically, in my best American accent.

My father Pat Hanna, known on the circuit as Pat McClusky, was a top class cabaret entertainer, highly rated amongst his peers. Seeing his talent played a big part in my desire to sing. I always thought, however biased my opinion, that he was just that extra bit special next to the other entertainers in his arena. Show business ran through his veins, the youngest of nine children, he was born into a travelling show in the south of Ireland. Performing was deeply ingrained into him as being a polished entertainer was a basic family value.

After leaving Ireland at the age of sixteen, my dad's performing career was established mainly in army bases and large variety clubs in the UK. Everywhere he went, people loved him. Perhaps this was what spurred me on in my dream. The thought of holding a microphone filled me with giddy anticipation.

The first album I ever owned was a Carpenters album – 'A Song For You'. Dad bought it from a local car-boot sale and although it was supposed to be for mum, that didn't quite work out. There was something special about Karen

Carpenter's voice. It took me elsewhere. It seemed like something so beautiful couldn't possibly originate from this world. For the next two years I listened to that album every time we got into the car. I knew every part, of every song.

And of course as I learned the songs I began to imitate the sounds and notes. My parents encouraged me as soon as I began to show interest. Yet doubt crept in. Though people often asked me to sing, I was suddenly nervous. What if my voice wasn't up to standard? What if they laughed at me?

I fell in love with singing

Singing always felt spiritual to me. I felt that no matter what might happen, it would be something I could always turn to, something outside of the norm that I could escape to if I was sad.

I had never been to church other than to attend weddings. I'd heard a bit about Jesus. Mum bought me the nativity on cassette tape and we sang hymns at school. I imagined that there might be a God, but I certainly didn't feel a connection with Him. I figured that the truth about life was something I'd be waiting till after death to find. I never imagined you could 'know' God in this life, unless you were some kind of religious nut.

I loved music all the way through school. My passion to one day be a singer made me seem a bit 'different' at times. I sang in front of my classmates once and was sure I'd impressed them. But they started to tease me, and my confidence began to shrink.

I was a high-maintenance, over-imaginative child. At night, whilst others kids my age were sound asleep, I was wide-awake, colouring in on the landing. When other kids were bouncing to life at 6:30 am to watch breakfast TV, I was being painfully coaxed out of bed with a piece of toast. I always dreamed of being a musician but my stage fright now made it seem impossible. I couldn't even imagine how I would face this fear, let alone enjoy being on the stage.

Though this was upsetting, I felt that giving up wasn't an option. I always had the feeling that there was a path marked out for me and that one-day I'd get to use my voice for something special.

the slippery slope...

As I went into Secondary school some new challenges emerged. I'd learned to appreciate my position at primary school. The new school seemed big, anonymous and institutional. The friends I'd made had gone to different schools, so I was beginning from social scratch, and didn't find it easy. I didn't excel in my subjects as I had in primary school. In the past I'd buried my head in study to enjoy school. Now I didn't feel so clever.

It seemed to me that during my first year at school, students began to split into very separate categories. The two main 'cliques' seemed to be those that would endure and remain focused through the tough patches, and the others who took struggle as a sign that they 'weren't good enough'. These kids would usually set out to make up their own rules at school.

After the simplicity of Primary school, searching for the right 'clique' and navigating the maze of corridors with my new timetable made me feel very lost. In this respect I was pretty much a normal teenager. Perhaps this is the point at which many teenagers become distant from their families and retreat to their bedrooms to listen to music and chat online. At that age, when your social life gets turned upside down, it can create a real sense of failure. The shame of

this failure can distance you from the people whose
approval you crave the most.

I could have taken on this challenge as an opportunity. But
instead I looked around at my peers, seeing that they had
everything 'together' and made a very unsound judgement.
I decided to go off the rails. I'd had enough. My grades
were average and I felt like just another face in the crowd.

Life naturally becomes difficult for all of us at times. As an
adult you can learn that life's serene momentum is often
broken up by struggles. We begin to learn that it produces
character and experience. As a teenager you don't have the
benefit of knowing there is light at the end of those tunnels
and don't always ask for advice when you should. When
senior school presented problems I began to look for an
easy escape route. I thought I'd give rebellion a try.

crazy days

You're all grown up now
And you've cut your pretty brown hair
We've come so far now, And I wouldn't be where I am,
if you hadn't **been there**

I'm not going to worry
If we made the **best of the time** we had
We've become somebody

Crazy days, crazy days What were we thinking of?
And though I'm glad I had those times with you
There's so much more to look forward to
A new life in the light,
now I'm following Him
Crazy days, crazy days, lived out in crazy ways
And thank the Lord we came through
For He is the life and truth
I walk by day, **not by night**, now I'm following Him
Now I'm following Him

So **bright eyed and pretty** now
I'm glad to have my picture taken with you
'Cos you look so much better now
So much happier and healthier too
Remember when we ran away
We didn't even last a day
Before we came home

And **we'd no need** to worry
Cos even though we drove our parents mad
They **still lent us** money

crazy days...

'for you were formerly darkness, but now you are
Light in the Lord; walk as children of Light'
Ephesians 5:8

What were we thinking of?

Roz was the little girl who lived up the road. We were
introduced by our mums as playmates. They had been good
friends for years even before I was born. Roz was a great
little girl. She had adorable long brown hair, big brown eyes
and as she was two years my senior I believed her to be the
oracle of all knowledge. She had lots of school friends
whilst I was still in playgroup and I loved going round to
her house. Being nine years younger then my next eldest
sibling I was always the only kid in my house so I loved it
when Roz came to play.

As she started school our mums didn't talk as much and
when I turned four I started school elsewhere. We only
really played together occasionally after that. I remember
the first time I saw her after her adult teeth had come
through. She looked so grown up!

It was only when I started Secondary school and we were
catching the same bus that we began to form a new
friendship. Our village bus stop was the farthest from
school, so we all had a good few miles to mess about
together on the bus. In summer it was great. We trampled

up and down the top deck, all the windows open, shirts untucked, shouting at cows as we passed fields. At first the older kids gave me the usual hassle for being new. But over time we began to hang out. They were two years older, which is obviously forever at Secondary school.

I started school with the best of intentions. The trip to WH Smiths for all the new improved stationary, the new shoes, shirts and school tie! It was supposed to be the beginning of a new era in academic brilliance. But almost immediately I didn't get on too well. My few close Primary buddies had dispersed to other schools. The new system of going from class to class, studying new subjects and being an anonymous face in the crowd, began to make me feel quite small and insecure.

Hanging out with the older kids from my village including Roz, made school easier to face. But being so much older, it didn't help much once we through the gates. Different classes, different timetable, different world.

I started to feel quite low. Whilst observing the new social systems in my school, I noticed that a handful of girls were involved in an exciting teacher-dodging camaraderie in the toilets. They were sharing cigarettes, passing them round and getting people to buy them with their lunch money. 'Finally', I thought. 'Something that might make school life a bit more exciting!'

When I've asked people why they started smoking they usually give a suave answer like – 'oh, I just fancied one with a drink when I turned twenty-one'. Or 'I used smoking to cope with exams and just carried on after I'd passed'. So maybe I'm the only one that was actually affected by 'peer pressure'. If that is the case then allow me to confess on behalf of anyone who doesn't feel they can.
Yes. This is it- the confession. I started smoking to look cool, to fit in and to make the teachers notice me.

For me and I'm guessing for many others, I went looking for temptation and dived into it. No self-respecting teenager wants to admit that they'd let other people dictate their behaviour. "Peer pressure? Me? NO way, I do what I want. No one TELLS me to". These are some things that may have come out of my mouth at the time. The words, 'peer pressure' make them cringe as a teenager. But when your happiness in school life seems to be under threat there's no telling what measures you'll take to defend it, despite how clever and capable you may be.

Looking back, I'm not sure I truly understood what peer pressure was. There was no one saying 'try this, try this' or 'everybody's doing it.' Or even 'if you do this, you'll look really cool'. In retrospect it was my own teenage insecurity that piled on the pressure. The need to fully connect with new people and the uncomfortable feeling of walking into a classroom and not having someone to sit with. Maybe that's why it seemed to sneak up on me, and why I was under the illusion that I could somehow control my journey through it. My appearances alongside the more 'adventurous' girls in the year group began to change things. I started to be noticed more and as a result began to gain some kind of confidence.

juicy fruit?

When we hear the word 'temptation' it can create a vivid picture. It often brings to mind the idea of delights that you aren't supposed to touch. There's a certain glamour to it. It brings to mind numerous ad campaigns for chocolate and lingerie. It creates the illusion that something delicious and tantalising is being withheld from us.

A typical ad campaign for a chocolate ice cream on your TV today might look something like this. A nervous woman in dull, conservative clothes suddenly has her sexy, inner-self broken loose by the experience of this new taste. She was boring and now she's exciting. She was wasting life on the shelf and now she's on the loose. She's been liberated by her indulgence. Our perception of freedom is clicked one notch further from rational for the sake of selling ice cream.

The fruit in the Garden of Eden looks so shiny in the pictures – something so irresistible that it couldn't be resisted. It fosters the illusion that there'll always be something better we could taste if only we'd break the rules a little. But as the story goes, the reality is different.

It's a story of how certain things are withheld from us because it's for the best, and learning not to choose them is an important part of our development. Parents keep toxic cleaning agents out of the reach of children for a reason don't they?

The fruit wasn't really a delicious juicy treat at all. It was a bitter dissatisfying fruit - not intended for eating. When the serpent came along and whispered in Eve's ear, he made her doubt what she'd been told by the one who loved her most. God had told her, that if she was to eat from this particular tree she would surely die, but with a bit of help from this unhelpful voice she forgot the truth.

As we watch shiny skinned couples having spontaneous sexual encounters to advertise perfume or jeans, their carefree abandon tells us we're 'missing out'. How easily we forget that this guidance isn't coming from people who care. It's not coming from forces that want to shape our society in a positive way. It's not coming from friends. It's coming from sales people trying to sell us clothes, ice cream and perfume.

Just like the woman in the familiar fruit story, we've been

given love driven warnings about how toxic our choices can be. But the unhelpful voice of the media tells us we should eat and drink what we want. We should do whatever makes us 'feel good' at the time.

freedom?

When I was feeling down as a teenager cigarettes became the thing I couldn't 'live' without. I was so hooked on the comfort brought by them. I loved my lighter and the snugly feeling of there being a good few left in the box, cracking the window slightly in my room and looking at the stars with the warm smoke going down to the depths of my lungs and curling out against the sky. I know this is not everyone's problem. Some of us just like to smoke. Some smokers are just addicted to nicotine. I was addicted to the comfort.

If I had an argument with someone I'd have a cigarette. If I was stressed or hormonal, cigarettes to the rescue! Getting rid of them meant less joy, and less fun. 'If I haven't got my little bad habit to keep me going through hard times what have I got'?

For so long I'd been learning that happiness could only come from doing whatever I wanted.

...That having a liberal attitude towards everything was giving me 'freedom'.

Perhaps this was all just a big shiny looking apple that was never going to gush sweetly onto my tongue. It was never going to bring me good health and a sense that all was well.

Young people in the UK have never had more social 'freedom' but despite this, statistics showed a marked increase in teen suicide between the seventies and nineties. One thing seems evident; all this social, 'freedom' is actually not providing the progress we might have hoped for. The joy is simply not there as we expected.

Faith is often used in marketing to represent a boring way of life. The occasional Christian character in a soap opera is painted as the butt of jokes, eccentric and unaccustomed to fun. The general impression is that a life given to God robs you of something.

If you give up sex, drinking, smoking etc. you'll be missing out on enjoyment. This life is so full of trials and pain that the suggestion of giving up any pleasurable habit seems hard to swallow.

Partying lifts your spirits.
Drugs offer a break from the norm.
Sex brings escapism.
Being able to do exactly what you want, and when is often the ultimate goal for our lives.

In the Bible Jesus uses these words: **"I have come that they might have life, and have it to the full,"** John 10:10.

How odd that Jesus would promise something like this whilst teaching that self-control and holiness were what our lives should be producing. It doesn't make sense somehow. Unless our whole view of joy and our whole perception of what actually makes us feel 'good' is somehow out of sync. What if we really don't *know* what makes us **truly** joyful?

Most people seem to find by trial and error that the simple things like taking a walk with their kids, preparing a good meal, or saving to afford their new car gives them real joy. It never seems to come from the recklessness that our world encourages. And as I found, it doesn't emerge from rebellion either.

13

Where am I going?

When I left school this question started to really trouble me.

Looking into the New Testament, we see how 'the disciples' dropped everything they were doing to follow this man, Jesus. They ditched all of their plans because they knew somehow that it was the right thing to. But you have to wonder - as normal young people did they ever ask themselves...

Where are we going?

Will we *ever* get there?

When it came to following Jesus, even the disciples were a little anxious about their route plan. In the book of John the disciple Thomas says,

"Lord, we don't know where you are going, so how can we know the way?" John 14:5

I'd been born into a family that had always supported me in my gifts. They'd always believed in me. Even more than that, I had a real sense of destiny built into my thinking. I believed there was a good life waiting somewhere for me. I was just so afraid I would never find it. I was afraid of being joyless in the meantime. So I bit into the apple and set out to take my place in that 'wrong crowd'.

The wrong crowd is not made up of 'bad' people. It's so easy to look at groups of young people under this judgmental view and miss a vital truth. Each young person making up the crowd has a burning need to belong, to know who they are and be loved.

Some were genuinely struggling with schoolwork. Some had
no support or encouragement coming from home, and had
never been shown a future worth working hard for. Some
were picked out by others to go along for the ride. Some
were just like me- **afraid to fade into the background.**

All of us were after one sought-after thing. **Joy.**
We were joy seeking in friendship, spontaneity, romantic
interest, from the excitement of being in a bit of trouble,
and even from basic substances like alcohol. Although I had
a sense that I was about to make some mistakes, being a
part of the wrong crowd looked deceptively like a lifeline.

In this daily focus of developing these friendships and
exploring new experiences, there seemed to be a good
reason to go to school.

As I joined these teenagers at school we got up to a lot of
'crazy' things. There was a lot of drinking, drugs and sex
going on within the group. It was normal for someone to
pass out and have to be looked after. It was acceptable to
hear about someone going 'all the way' (or a good part of
it). It wasn't as acceptable to be well behaved. I'm not sure
why. But perhaps it came from watching clever students do
well, feeling threatened and not seeing how else we could
be different and special. A lot of teenagers just didn't see
the point in all this struggle.

I was a little confused about the importance of obedience in
school. Growing up in a world that didn't altogether make
much sense to me, meant there wasn't much appeal in
joining it. There was a deep sense of hopelessness
ingrained in my thinking.

Looking at the news, all I could see was a decline in morals.

You grow up in a society where the older generations can't tell you enough how things were somehow 'better' in their day.

I wasn't sure I was going to find joy in being good

At the first sense of trial in school, I 'cut off my nose to spite my face' and withdrew from achieving. As I fell further behind with studies I grew more passive. I was becoming more noticeable and well liked among the students and I drew closer to this as it provided my security. As more opportunities to try new things and break more rules arose, I took the leap to invest in my social life. I had completely lost sight of my dreams, and of the purposes I'd felt in my life. The added stress of making my parents despair changed my self-image too. It used to be that I had trouble fitting in at school, but was always the apple of my parents' eye. Now I was the life and soul of the party, the class clown, and my parents couldn't go a day without some stress or heartache to do with my schooling or out-of-school exploits.

It just seemed that I couldn't be both good and happy. This is where the shiny seductive apple proved bitter and hollow. I was shown something, an easy route to a better life. **And it was an illusion.**

the song...

Perhaps my worst offence against my parents during those 'crazy days' was running away. After attending a party at a friend's house that ended in all kinds of disaster, my parents grounded me. Roz and I made the playful decision to run away from home. We packed our bags and began trekking across the fields towards our nearest town.
As it got into the early hours of that morning and I knew my parents would be panicking I began to feel ill with remorse. I will never forget the fraught look on mum's face as she picked us up from the police station. In hindsight, I know I had every intention of returning home before long. It was all just 'fun and games', but we were very lucky not to come up against any real danger.
I wrote the song 'crazy days' shortly after I found that Roz

was going to be a mum. I looked at my friend, grown up from being a cute child – through the fire of our teens and out the other side. Roz had turned out beautiful, unscathed and was about to enter into motherhood. I began to believe that God had done a great work of protection in our lives.

Many young people aren't as lucky. I can recall people that started on hard drugs and are still there, even people who lost their lives to it. I know there are lots of bright beautiful young people that make one wrong choice and pay for it with their lives.

For whatever reason, I'm here to tell this story. And I had an opportunity to share it with you in these chapters. In Jesus a hand was stretched out to me and I took it. This was the hope I'd been looking for. **It held the joy I'd been looking for.**

There was always an inner voice of reason that I was ignoring, sometimes more than others. But God kept trying to reach me. He was knocking at the door of my heart for years.

He was there every moment of that journey. He delivered me out of some terrible situations and He's been miraculously dealing with those things from my past since the moment I came into relationship with Him. It's a story I'm excited to be telling.

'It's not God' you might think. **It's just a 'new leaf'.**

I had often tried to turn over a new leaf in my old life, to start 'afresh'. As I turned twenty I had a boyfriend, plenty of friends and was slowly gluing together a career in music. But I found that although the senior school days were behind me, I couldn't stave off the teenage drama. Issue after issue would arise. I couldn't stop making bad decisions and I couldn't catch hold of that childhood happiness I longed for. I felt sort of old and worn out when I was barely out of my teens. I still didn't have any direction. Everything I stood for was proving itself false.

They say a leopard never changes his spots and try as I did, I couldn't change mine. After choosing to derail myself there was no undoing my decision.

I have been given new life since I chose 'following Him' as my direction. I have that **full** life the world seems to be chasing. There's no disappointing apple involved. It has come from knowing His love and understanding why I'm alive.

I can rest in knowing my actions are guided.
It's full because I know,

'in all things God works for the good of those who love him, who have been called according to his purpose'.
Romans 8:28

It's full because I know that if I follow God's loving guidance, I'll never walk away from a person I'm crazy about and feel used. I'll never have to fear unwanted pregnancy or worry about contracting a sexually transmitted infection. There really is a better way.

No self-help technique or idea had achieved any lasting success in my life. A healing transformation took place when I opened my heart to knowing Him. It revisited the parts of it that were completely screwed up from my teens and made them feel new again.

I got back that part of me I thought I'd put away with my Barbie dolls and the Easter bunny. Jesus somehow transformed everything in my life.

There's only one truth
what's true is true
I found the truth and the truth is You, Jesus
There's only one voice
I'm listening to
I found the way and the way is You, Jesus
I wanna tell the world
how You gave me life
And you are everything that's right, Jesus

I wanna see
Your name lifted high
as angels wings, So that all the earth rejoices
and all of heaven sings
Now I found my way to You I'm
never going back

Wanna be ready
Ready for the day of the Lord
Coming back to save us
Coming back to save us all
He **doesn't care** what
you've done wrong
Or where you've come here from
So give him your praises
'Cos He is the Lord

Are you ready? Are you ready?
Are you ready for the day of the Lord?
Are you ready? Are you ready?
for the day of the Lord?

one truth...

'I am the way the Truth and the Life. No one comes to the father except through Me'. John 14:16 (NIV)

who can I trust?

I've always been listening for A VOICE. Something to guide me, a voice of reassurance and wisdom. After a certain age, I wasn't willing to follow my parents' voice. So I looked for guidance elsewhere. Christianity wasn't the obvious choice for me. So from being around thirteen, I started to search for this guidance in other places.

During my 'skiving' days, I found myself wandering into a pagan shop. The owner was in her mid forties, very glamorous with long fair hair, bright lips and black lacy clothes. The people who owned the shop were very welcoming and offered to 'read my aura' straight away. They offered to identify my 'spirit guide' and lead me through visualising and describing a person I could imagine. I couldn't really feel anything, but I constructed an idea in my head and went along with things. These people really interested me by their willingness to believe in something deeper than the surface of life. They were more than happy to entertain me until 3:30 when I could get the bus home and pretend I'd been to school.

From that point onwards I became interested in anything from tarot, fairy and angel cards, to the ancient medicines of the Americas, past lives and crystal healing. I consulted Horoscopes, psychics and resorted to new-age treatments. I always had quite an open mind.

I'm not sure what makes the difference between a cynic, a believer and all the people in between. Whether it's upbringing, experience, personality type, or a mixture of everything, I don't know. There are plenty of books on the subject. But by taking a quick cross-section of the many people who walk this Earth we can see that belief in God, or a lack thereof has no direct correlation with intelligence.

Both in and out of 'church' you can find doctors, scientists, teachers, lawyers, philosophers, athletes and musicians - highly functional people with sensible upright lives. So are all Christians desperate, traumatised, brainwashed, death-fearing tambourine bashers? I may have suspected so at one time, but as I made friends with more and more people who claimed to love Jesus I found it was mainly the opposite. They all seemed to be joyful, driven, passionate and peaceful people.

Class, race, or country of origin may play some part in what you believe. But I found that people from all walks of every imaginable life follow Christ. I heard how all over the world many are turning from the religion they were raised in to follow Jesus. I figured that if they're not crazy, pathetic or dim there must be something to all this.

As a twenty year old, singer/bartender I'd thrown together a chaotic belief system from the world's buffet of beliefs and religions.

We live in a world where you can buy a Buddha figurine in the home-ware section of the local supermarket. The lights in the town centre change month to month to accommodate the traditions of each faith.

Truth?

everything happens for a reason...

Perhaps it was the music in my life that made my mind open a little. I felt a sense of destiny in my desire to write songs and sing. It seems dreams often provoke a sense of destiny in people. You may feel like you're destined to dance, or have children. Maybe you feel destined to run a business. Many people, who don't believe in God, will profess a belief in destiny. We casually use phrases like:

- 'It's meant to be'
- 'Everything happens for reason'
- 'It'll be all right in the end'.
- 'When it's right, you'll know'.

Although I didn't always believe in a certain God, I always had a loose belief in these ideas.

Spirituality is integrated into the practice of medicine in the UK. Nurses must ensure that each patient's spiritual needs are taken into account in their plan of care. So even the medical profession regard people as being spiritual, regardless of what they do or don't believe. It's broadly accepted that there is a spiritual dimension to humanity, whatever form that might take.

If we delve deeper it's supposed by many that there is some kind of spiritual realm, connections between people, intuition between close friends or relatives, bad 'vibes'

24

when you walk into a room; peaceful places and spiritually 'muddy' places. The more I allowed myself to be open to such ideas, the more heightened my awareness of them became. Not surprisingly this led to more questions.

As I went through the knock-backs and letdowns inevitable for an ambitious musician, my life would play through my mind as a sort of romantic movie where the girl is meant for something **more**. There are plenty of shallow reasons to desire fame and many reasons to seek success that are born out of insecurity. But I began to wonder, 'could it be that there's a fundamental cause for this?'

Deep down, I just wanted to give my life to a memorable cause. I wanted my life to count for something.

I entered a TV competition at the age of seventeen. By this point I had made countless demo tapes of my own and collaborated on several 'sure-fire hit' projects that hadn't come off. Finally my show-reel disk had been chosen from thousands for a local televised competition. It was every bit as dramatic as it looks on screen. They came to my door with a camera crew and put me on live regional TV the following week singing my song. Though it seemed like a dream coming true, I felt unready. I didn't quite feel I'd reached that point of facing the world. First prize was performing at a large pop festival but I didn't feel ready for that. Nevertheless, as loving family, friends, the people from local pubs and post-offices assured me, I was slowly convinced it was a one horse race. I gave it a good shot, and it went well.

Later on as I sat, drunk and sobbing in the bathroom cubicle of my local nightclub toilets after 'graciously' losing on live TV, some things went through my head. Though I wasn't a Christian, oddly they were part of a dialogue with God. I was having a bit of a go at Him.

'Why? Why have I got this desire in me if it's not going to happen?' I was dealing with what felt like a brick wall, which I'd been up against every step of the way so far.

From somewhere inside me a response to my question came. Perhaps it was my survival instinct. But I'm sure now that God was guiding me too. *'Keep going - never give up. There is something planned for you. Never give up.'*

As a child I supposed God was real and I even used to pray sometimes before bed. But the God they taught us about at school disappeared for me around the same time as Father Christmas. If anything remained it was a latent longing to believe, or a mild superstition. I didn't really know how to pray and it began to feel pointless. I would list all the things worth praying for and say 'Amen' at the end. It became a bit like a worn out workout video. I was bored of doing the same routine. I wasn't feeling God there, so I thought He must be somewhere else.

I think I've always considered myself cleverer than I am. Part of me thought I was working out the real truth, all by myself... a brand new truth. I thought that if Christianity *were* truth then I would have already believed it! It didn't seem to have the answers and it didn't allow me the lifestyle that I enjoyed. I was under the impression that it was based on a big old book written in a different language that supported ancient traditions, such as women being less important than men. I thought that surely faiths like Buddhism were more peaceful. Or perhaps the ancient beliefs of the Americas were worth considering? I loved the music of panpipes and paintings of handsome old Indians with white wolves sitting beneath silver moons.

So as categories go I fitted into the, 'I don't really believe in God but I do believe in something' category.

I am the way the Truth and the Life. No one comes to the Father except through me.

I would occasionally pray when something went wrong but I had begun to mould God into something that suited my ideas better. This left me with some burning questions and a feeling of growing confusion about life.

the new-age thing...

In my late teens, (post rebellion) I started to further investigate spirituality, seeking something that might make me feel more healthy and positive. I felt I should give my spiritual self some attention.

After school I'd spent nearly all my strength on trying to create a musical career. I was trying to get someone to believe in me as much as I did. Though I knew there was lots of work to be done in my development I just wanted someone to see the gold in me.

I was introduced to a series of books about something called 'Angel Therapy'. These books recognised the existence of angels and how we could share our every day lives with them, calling on them for the simplest of problems. I became very involved in this and began to spend money on my interest.

One book was actually constructed like an A-Z of spiritual masters to call on. Each even had a short list of relevant problems to consult them on. Many well-known 'masters' were there, including Jesus. Pushing to find some peace I kept following the instructions of this new age guru author but only found myself becoming increasingly lost. The more I believed, the more unanswered questions I had. No one seemed to have any answers. Not my life, my health or my heart was changing for the better.

meeting Jesus...

It was around this time when an acquaintance I'd met on my musical travels became a Christian. His name was Roo and we'd been introduced at an open-mic night in Preston some weeks before. I was so impressed by his musical skill and freedom that we soon began working together on material. He was a cool guy with a lot going for him, and finding he'd become a Christian was a huge surprise, as he far from fit my mental stereotype. Spending time with him kicked off an even deeper curiosity about the meaning of life.

There was a tangible sense of change in me as I went back to my song-writing roots, and began to feel more artistic again. As we chatted on subjects like life purpose, relationships and spirituality, his newfound views were very challenging to me. He was waiting until marriage before having sex and seemed uninterested in getting drunk. He always made an effort to think of others before himself and I found myself intrigued. I think above all, it wasn't merely the abstinence that impressed me; it was the spark of life within my new friend that seemed to fulfil and excite him without the need for those things which I had relied on for my enjoyment of life. Even more impressively, I quickly found that he wasn't the only one of his kind. I soon met numerous Christians my age with similar intriguing qualities. They loved life, they followed God, and they had time for me.

As I began to learn about Christianity I felt as though something was trying to prevent me moving forward towards it. It was as if I was on the brink of some important discovery, yet I might also be on the brink of ruin. I was clinging onto my career for some kind of breakthrough and finding myself less and less spiritually grounded. As the ideas that I'd been clinging to were daily losing clout I began to question whether I believed anything at all. I was feeling quite confused as to where to put my trust. I had considered myself something of an expert on the spiritual realm. But Roo's passion and lifestyle were so far removed from mine. There was authority in his conviction and I began to envy the light and peace that was shining out from his life, which like mine had once been far from holy.

For all my 'enlightenment' I hadn't been able to take care of my relationships or myself. In fact I like so many young people, had been the primary source of destruction in my own life. Roo's life was boldly reflecting the truth he believed. Could it be that there was a *real* truth? One that couldn't be bent? The problem with my spirituality was that it wasn't built on anything solid, but was flexible and colourable. Anyone could add to it what he or she liked. There was nothing to challenge me and thus, nothing there to change me.

By this time I was considering becoming a Christian if only to spend more time with Christians! I caught in them a glimpse of hope and I felt as though I was moving towards it like a moth to flame. I was just so afraid to let go of my otherworldly views. The thought of changing so much frightened me and **what if I could no longer be a singer?** What I would wear, talk and sing about - were all questions.

After a recording session with my friend Andy, he took me aside to talk to me about my musical career. He said something to the tune of *'you have to put your plans in God's hands. Things might not turn out the way you expect, but it will be better than trying to make something happen in your own strength.'* I was nervous about surrendering my dreams. They'd been my only source of hope for so long, the idea of risking them terrified me. And there was another problem; I hadn't committed myself to Jesus. I hadn't let go of myself and I didn't really understand even how to begin doing that.

After some time of being around these clean, life-filled people, I was beginning to feel aware of how old and tired I felt. Then I found myself at a church meeting.

It wasn't like any church meeting I'd ever been too. There was no one dressed up, no liturgy and no hymns. Just a guy and his electric guitar. My reason for going that night was more about proving I wasn't afraid, than anything. But as people around me were letting go I was suddenly struck with how afraid *I* was to let go. Then the man with the guitar began singing a song which had the following words repeated at several points; *'Cast all your burdens upon the Lord, 'cos Jesus cares, He cares for you.'*

It was at this point that I found myself praying. I was responding to an altar call from God.

A strange mix of beliefs had confused me. I had prayed to the debt angel and asked St. Michael to help with my broken printer (based on one new-aged author's advice). Next to all this, the resonance in God's story astounded me with its authenticity. It even explained the very need in me to search. Irrespective of the thousands of years since the story began, the wisdom I found in the Bible was profoundly relevant to my situation. And finally, the Character of God was becoming clearer to me. It blew my mind. I found that if went far beyond any God whose traits I could idealise.

other faiths...

I remember the discussions we would have in R.E at school.
We studied the basic principles of each faith. It was usually
more about traditions than anything else.
When we discussed Christianity we generally agreed that if
we followed the teachings of Jesus the world would be
sorted. With this in mind it seemed that Christianity could
be a clever invention, designed to keep the world in some
kind of order. But the more I allowed myself to recognise
the foolishness of man and the wisdom of God, the less I
could imagine my species dreaming up these principles.

I suspected at first that Biblical teaching was like the
cataloguing of everything moral, compiled as an instruction
manual to keep us in line. As I allowed my heart to open for
the first time since Santa disappeared, I began to see that
the story of God offered a deeper explanation. Something
big enough to overshadow the idea that Christianity was an
invention.

From the experience of the wisdom of Jesus transforming
my mind, heart and life I know that only by accepting Jesus
into my heart fully could I begin to lay aside my own idea of
what was right. My own version of what was right seemed
to rob me of so much. I came to a place where my desire
was to be led by true wisdom.

Many psychologists believe that your sense of right and
wrong comes from a mixture of nature and nurture. But
nobody seems to be able to answer the question, how did
morality begin? Who set the precedent? Where does that
lust to do right, (which seems exclusive to the human race),
actually come from?

From my Religious Studies classes at school I had drawn

the conclusion that religious people were generally good, whatever they believed, and those without such guidance were generally rougher around the edges.

I had decided that all religions had perfect 'morals'. It's hard to say if this view is sensible without fine tooth-combing every religion. Moreover, without some kind of moral code it's difficult to define what is right and wrong in the first place. But what I began to learn as I entertained Christianity a bit more was this ... Only the Bible contained the historically attested account of this Prince Of Peace - a person who willingly suffered a painful death although He was perfect, to die in place of me. Jesus was only the Son of God in one religion. Only in Christianity did I find the option of new beginning and the promise of transformation. Only Jesus promised to heal my past and bring me into a relationship with God.

The offer was on the table, and as I continued to seek out answers I began to consider that I might find this Truth I'd been seeking in the person of Jesus.

the song...

I began to write 'One Truth' as a simple, fun song. After being introduced to the exciting world of gospel music my head was flooding with those uplifting vibes and I was keen to draw on them for my new material. Washing up one afternoon in my new Sheffield home, I was considering the concept of 'Truth". I used to believe that truth was relative. In-keeping with my pick-and-mix ideas about the meaning of life, I'd chosen to believe that truth is made up. You select what sits well with your belief system. You open yourself up only to what fits your perception of life.

As I accepted Jesus I began to consider the possibility that perhaps Truth was more like the deeper twin sister of fact. It's there, like a rock in the middle of the road. How you feel about it doesn't cause it to disappear. If you look at our world and consider how and why it came to be, there must be an answer. Either Christianity is True or false.

The last few years have been a journey for me, of travelling across that solid, unchanging rock in the road. It wasn't in my plan. This reality wasn't a part of the landscape I was used to. Walking along a rocky path, you can't just blink your eyes and recreate a smoother one for your own convenience. Perhaps up until this point I'd been quite successful in avoiding this rock in the road, looking for any kind of short cut. But the alternative routes seemed to be leading me nowhere.

Jesus claimed to be 'The Way, the Truth and the Life.'
In the verses to One Truth, I wanted to take this verse and apply it to my 21st century story.

I've accepted that this Truth is indeed true. I've found the Truth and the Truth is Jesus.
I've accepted that He is the path I need to take. Else I'd be going round in circles, looking for the answers without Him.

Finally, I've accepted that true **life** is in Him, and I've never felt more alive

 father

I need You now more than
I've needed You before
And though I need You everyday
Today I really need You more,
The walls are closing in
My thoughts are spiralling, But I know You're waiting
to lift me up

Father can You hear me
I'm knocking I'm knocking
I'm knocking at Your door
Praying You wont let me **fall apart**
Father I need You near me
I'm falling, I'm falling,
I'm falling to the floor
Giving You all my broken heart

So I will trust in what You're calling me to do
So when the rain falls down
You want me to rely on You
To learn the meaning of
What it truly is to love Your name
I'll never be the same

Father can You hear me
I'm knocking I'm knocking
I'm knocking at Your door
Praying You wont let me **fall apart**
Father I need You near me
I'm falling, I'm falling,
I'm falling to the floor
Giving You all my broken heart

God I know You can hear me
You **always** keep Your promises;
I'm putting my life into Your hands
I will not stumble no I will not fear
I'm humbled by Your faithfulness
No eye **has seen** what's in Your plans

father...

Ask and it will be given to you; seek and you will find; knock and the door will be opened to you.
(Matthew 7:7 NIV)

so how do I know it's true?

When I became interested in Christianity, a friend of mine coaxed me along to a church service or two. I heard this verse from the book of Matthew used often. It's such a simple concept. It made getting what you need or want sound so simple. I have to say that at the time, the verse made me question the very idea of God.

I'd never experienced miraculous provision. I'd certainly not received all the things I had dreamt of in my life. I could stretch my imagination to the idea of a 'hands off' God, a kind of energy who had no direct involvement with me. But to imagine a God who was personal; suppliant of my every need and who truly cares about the details of my life; my worries, relationships, money and even catching the right bus, I couldn't see any evidence of it and it just didn't seem to make sense. If I broke down the verse it seemed quite easy to disprove it.

ask...and it will be given to you

I had asked for things in the past that I'd not received.
I recalled times where desperation had led me to try

praying. When relatives had been sick or I'd had troubles at school. I couldn't see how God had answered my prayers.

seek...and you shall find

I had wondered often about the existence of God and not had any clear answers. I'd explored other faiths and ideas and not been aware of any clear guidance.

knock...and the door will be opened to you

I had not yet found Jesus Himself. Though I'd never truly requested that God take over my life, I felt if were a door to go though then God would have invited me in before now. I'd never felt anything significant happening. It felt in fact like I'd been searching (be it in the wrong places) for my whole life and never found the God my Christian friends were giving their lives to. Why could they clearly see Him in their minds when I could hardly imagine Him in mine? What was it that made Him so personal to them? I could have concluded that it was merely, 'not for me'. The temptation to write God off was there. But I was finding it hard to let go of that longing to share in what was giving them so much life.

So the **asking, seeking and knocking** idea was key in my unbelief.

I'd asked for God to do things
I'd looked for God in several places
and I assumed there was no real need to knock.

But in truth, I'd never really approached this God, the God whom Jesus had died to reconcile me to. The God of the Bible, I'd never really asked Him into my life on *His* terms. I realised that God can only be God and I can't make Him bend the rules for my habits.

So one very key element in the story had to take place. I had to take God at His word and give Him my life.

I took God up on His challenge.

I was certainly uncomfortable the night I was standing beside my Christian friends and saw them raising their arms to worship 'God'. It was just so bold, and if I didn't know better I would have said they were mentally unsound. I may have been able to half accept the idea of God: superstitiously avoiding blasphemy, just in case. I'd always enjoyed singing along to 'Silent Night' at Christmas; it's a tradition after all. But raising your arms seemed like a whole new level. Whatever was going on here, these folks were very into it!

This wasn't on the same level as putting on a clean shirt and attending a building as a family tradition, or those complicated, (dare I say, sometimes boring) hymns with words I didn't understand. It wasn't a group of dull people 'being on their best behaviour' It *was* a group of people whom up until this moment had appeared sane, functional, exciting and intriguing, now passionately engaging in something I'd never really seen before. It seemed like this 'God' was shaping their lives and their minds into something vastly different.

I never expected to find 'switched on', 'trendy' young people that were willing to make examples of themselves for something totally contrary to their culture. This was something that went against the grain of what the world was teaching them daily. No TV or film screen, no mainstream radio, news or entertainment, seemed to be inspiring this.

After *my* experience of being a teenager, I was cynical that this kind of teenager even existed! But here they were all the time - in church, serving Jesus.

In this meeting, people were praising and letting go of their inhibitions, I was intimidated and inspired with their abandon.

They were dancing as though nobody was watching.
They were shouting out the deepest thoughts in their heart.
They were letting go of their 'street cred' to give thanks to the Creator.

There was one other small thing that made some impression on me. If I closed my eyes and listened to the people singing around me, it sounded like angels. The praise of these ordinary people sounded, well, heavenly.

I've often told people that during that meeting two unexpected things happened.

Something of God's heart for me was revealed in a song

It was something I needed to hear. Something no one in the room could ever have known I needed to hear ... *'cast all your burdens, upon the Lord, cos Jesus cares, He cares for you'.*

I pushed though a barrier

As people were worshipping, waving their arms around and crying out, I felt the urge to bolt for the door. I didn't want to be rude, and I didn't want my friends to think I was running from God. Then I began to wonder - am I running from God? It was at this point that I made a decision to press in. Instead of staying in my comfort zone I made a choice to challenge my own thinking.
A faintly familiar voice in my heart asked...

What are you afraid of?
If this really was just a bunch of harmless 'Christians' living out their faith why was I having such a dramatic response? Then another question came to me...

Why are you really here?
I'd been coasting around Christians for a couple of months by this point, wanting to share in their experience but afraid to lay down my conceptions and the opinions that twenty years in the world had given me. I began to get a sense that I'd been somehow guided to this place and I was now being given an opportunity to make a response.

I'd had a revelation. 'Cast all your burdens upon the Lord. Jesus cares for you'. It felt like time to make a response. **So my response was**: if you do care for me Lord - if this is true, I want to know you like these people do.

Somewhere in that meeting I realised that I was desperate to be parented. I'd pushed my own parents away in my teens and I made every effort to disarm my teachers of their authority over me at school. I'd spent the following few years trying to look after myself or find someone who would. I got a sense that God was offering me a place to go and maybe this was what I'd needed from the start.

When I looked at how dry and fruitless my life had become in spite of all I felt I could achieve, I realised I must be 'running on empty'. I was functional. I thought I was probably working my way towards some kind of contentment. But I was growing at snail-pace for one simple reason: I'd been living without the things I needed. Like a cactus can go for years without any fresh water, I was alive but slowly running out of life. And I definitely didn't seem to be growing.

the orphan option...

I moved out of my parents' house unofficially at the age of eighteen, staying with different people in different cities, mostly to pursue my music career. Although I was eating well and looking after my basic needs, I had begun to function without a few very important things. I was going without,

direction

discipline,

leadership

and mostly peace.

I had moved out of my parents' house emotionally long before moving out officially, perhaps even as I became a teenager. When I decided I knew best and I wanted to do things my way, I opted out of being parented. As a result I forfeited the security of knowing I was being guided.

Psalm 23 begins,

'The Lord is my Shepherd I shall not want'.
The closing line of this well loved psalm is;

'Surely goodness and love will follow me all the days of my life. And I will dwell in the house of the Lord forever.'

This is just one example of the many promises God was making to provide a Home for me **forever.** I felt like it was time for me to stop running, and go home.

Many of us choose the 'orphan option'. I've known people cut off their parents because of painful childhood memories. Many of my school friends chose their own way over their parents' guidance. Some just wanted desperately to prove they could make it on their own.

Even without any difficult personal issues, we all eventually have to go into the world unaccompanied. It's never simple. It makes such perfect sense when you realise, you can live in God's house **forever**.

That night, nobody in the room was calling me forward. I stepped towards God and entered into the place where the barrier between my ears and His voice could be taken away.

Now I could review how I'd misunderstood the verse about asking, seeking and knocking.

Ask and it shall be given to you.
Before that moment I had never asked God, to come into my life.

Have you asked for God to lead you?
Have you been asking for some other god to lead you, perhaps a god that you can compromise with a bit?

The problem there is no other god could make this promise. Have you ever approached the living God from whom this promise comes?

It seems so simple now, but until this point I'd never uttered the words, 'God, please show me you're there. Please have my life'.

Seek and you shall find...
I had never really looked for, 'Jesus.'

Have you ever been shopping without really knowing what you're looking for? You know you need a new outfit for this occasion but you don't really know what it's going to be? How much easier is it to find if you KNOW what you're looking for? It certainly narrows your vision and sharpens your eyes.

When you search for something you've lost, you begin to visualise it in your mind. Sometimes if you're picturing the wrong thing you wont see it, even when it's right in front of you. Looking for your diary whilst on a phone call, you can search and search but not see that it's right there on the desk. **You're seeking but you don't find.**

Until that night I wasn't seeking Him. I was seeking an answer that suited my ideas, but I wasn't looking for Him. Sometimes the Truth isn't what we think we want it to be. But if you want the Truth, you have to be prepared for it to offend you, for it to change your life and direction. For it to influence your mind in a new way.

Joan Osborne asks in her number one hit 'What if God was one of us?'

'If God had a face, what would it look like?
And would you want to see
If seeing meant that you would have to believe?'

The truth is, I was never really looking for Jesus. I wasn't ready to see Him. It would mean that I would have to believe **and that I'd have to change.**

When my Christian friends began to tell me about Jesus, when I saw something so powerful at work in their lives and when the song in the worship meeting revealed something of God to me, I began to truly seek Him.

Knock and the door shall be opened...
I had not yet made a physical step towards God.

To knock on a door you have to step up, make a fist and stretch out your arm. This was the first time I'd humbled myself to stand before God and approach Him. This was the first time I'd I knocked. And He opened the door. When I uttered that simple prayer in my heart, something happened. I'll rest my testimony there for a second.

the song...

The song *Father* is about having a broken heart. I wrote the song whilst I was sitting alone in my parents' living room, being broken-hearted. I had started to get to know God. But it didn't stop me feeling pain or being confused about the direction my new life was going to take. My eyes had been opened to some truths that I wasn't so keen to hear. But those truths freed me to move forward. I didn't want to give up on the relationship I was in at the time, but I knew it was the right thing to do, so I was just hurting, and taking it to God. It was a very simple song to write.

Once you've given your life to Jesus and the door has been opened and you want to live in Him and see His Kingdom come, your heart will begin to align with His. The things you ask for and seek come into line with His plan. You'll ask for things that make sense for you and also for Him, because you are within each other.

God has been faithful to the letter in everything since I asked Him in. When you live in 'truth' the truth begins to prove itself. It starts to soak into your life like no pursuit of instant gratification has ever done. With God proving true to this challenging word about prayer, the whole Bible seemed to have much more credibility to me.

I have a relationship with the God of my Christian friends. There is no longer a barrier between my ears and His voice.

You may feel desperate; as though you're 'knocking, knocking, knocking,' and no one's answering. You're demanding, wanting the fulfilment of that promise in the book of Matthew.

If you're seeking God's Kingdom first...

Knock and,

The door to healing from your past hurt **will be opened.**

The door to being parented **will be opened.**

The door to your new home **will be opened...and you can live there all your days.**

Maybe you've been praying for the same things over and over but you are yet to see them materialise.

This is what God says:

'Do not be anxious about anything, but in everything, by prayer and petition, with thanksgiving, present your requests to God.' Philippians 4:6 (NIV)

We have to have faith and dedication in the practice of asking, seeking, and knocking

When I began to take God at His word and began to see the fulfilment of that promise over and over again in my life, I began to learn that I must believe this consistently.

The response I felt when I approached god through this sing, was that although my pain may still be there, I know God can hear my requests. I know He always keeps His promises.

He is always faithful and His plans are perfect. I don't always see or understand what He's doing. Sometimes it seems like He's taking me the scenic route to the destination He's promised. But He keeps His promises, and I'm choosing to trust that we will arrive.

new song

Lord Help me
deal with this frustration
Forgive me for my lack of patience
Whole world of useless information
It's not hard **to break** my concentration
La dada dada dada dada dada da
Take the wood from my eyes so I can see again

But **stop** me looking
For a face to fill an emptiness that's gone
There's no call to stretch this season on
If I grow weary
I will **cling** to You -
You're the rock I stand upon
I'm tired of singing apathy
And You deserve
a new song

Don't like the feeling when I lose control
I'm **reminded** of the me I let go
Not good at coping with the tension
I'm calling for **Your** intervention
Take the **wood** from my eyes so I can see again

But **stop** me looking
For a face to fill an emptiness that's gone
There's no call to stretch this season on
If I grow weary
I will **cling** to You -
You're the rock I stand upon
I'm tired of singing apathy
And You deserve
a new song

You say no weapon formed against me
No fear or death shall separate me from You
Yours is the victory

new song...

'Good people, cheer God!
Right-living people sound best when praising.
Use guitars to reinforce your Hallelujahs!
Play his praise on a grand piano!
Invent your own new song to him;
give him a trumpet fanfare.'
Psalm 33: 1-3 (The Message)

time to change my tune

So I prayed in my heart for God to reveal himself to me.
I thought in the back of my mind that if nothing happened,
I would simply write Christianity off. But even the dot of
belief I'd had seemed to be enough because the next day,
something amazing began to happen. Something had taken
place, and it was more than noticeable.

I awoke feeling somehow 'different'. It felt like there was
something to get up for. I suddenly felt intrigued to read
what Jesus had to say. I had a New Testament that had
been handed out in an assembly at school. I'm sure the
assembly had a message about Jesus, though I can't
remember anything of it. All I remembered was that it was
there in a bottom draw in my bedroom.

I had a group job interview that day and I had breezed
through it feeling warm and light and like I wanted to be a
blessing and a 'cheering up' to the other candidates. I felt

strangely that I wanted to share what I was feeling with them.

The interview went well and I left with the job. There was a long bus journey ahead so I pulled out the little red book again to pass the time. I kept on reading - I was gripped. There had been a few times when I'd flicked through this dated looking thing and the words had washed over me blankly. Now something different was happening.

As I read these verses with the same interest I would have at one time poured over my horoscopes, the Gospels came to life. Line after line this God (that other people seemed to know and I had always doubted), began to speak to me. He spoke about my life, the things I had to change and deal with, and above all, His power, His love and His very real presence. There was something oddly lifelike about the words as they answered questions the moment I was considering them.

My heart filled with hope and childlike optimism. There was a feeling that despite all my mistakes, and the damage of my past, I was no longer doomed to become more disillusioned and jaded.

I was absorbed in the Gospel of John at the back of the bus on the way to my sister's house. Suddenly someone knocked hard at the window beside me as though to distract me. I jumped about a foot from the seat! I barely saw who did this but the experience put me on edge. I couldn't be sure whether or not he'd seen that I was reading the Bible. But I had a sense that something intense was going on in my life. There was some kind of tremendous power in the book I was holding in my hands.

I shared the experience with my sister when I got to her house. She seemed fairly interested in my new faith, though not entirely sold. As I mentioned in my notes on 'One

Truth' a number of spiritual fads had made their way in and out of my life. We'd always had chats about these and searched ideas together, but I don't think my family was prepared for the changes Christianity was about to make in me.

Something had definitely taken place the night of the church meeting. After accepting Jesus the way had become clear, the dust had been blown out of my ears, and I could finally feel and hear what God thought of my life.

Over the following days I began to notice that I was reacting to things differently. TV programs with graphic violence and sex scenes suddenly seemed difficult to watch. I felt I was becoming re-sensitised. It just didn't sit right with me anymore.

I was being increasingly drawn to **purity**. Watching certain things felt like stuffing myself with poisonous sweets or junk food -just plain bad for me.

finding a new rhythm...

It wasn't easy. I recall first going to church. It was something like a week after I'd given my life to Jesus and I'd spent that time trying to come to terms with such things as heaven and hell. It seems so simple now, but at the time I was afraid.

When you think about it - would you be afraid if you found out there was a God? If you've grown up in church then it might not have the same shock to you. But when this God that you've heard so many stories about becomes real, it's something else. Suddenly, the reality of what that means, hits you hard. There's a whole story playing out around you that starts to come into focus. There's a plan, and you're in it. You begin to wonder how you missed it all this time.

I panicked a little at first. There was so much to take in like, 'who will the *new* me be? What if she's boring, what if she can't follow her dreams anymore. What if she's losing it?!'

During that first week I went from being pleasantly intrigued to being quite distressed. **God being real was going to change *everything*.**

The first thing that happened was I became single. The fear of being alone had been holding me in a relationship where neither of us was happy. In the days that followed my decision to follow Jesus I felt God give me a firm nudge in the direction of freedom from this.

I knew it was time to put my trust in God's plan for my life. I found a verse in my New Testament shortly after, that says this;

'Submit yourselves, then, to God. Resist the devil, and he will flee from you. Come near to God and he will come near to you'. James 4:7 (NIV)

It was time for me to stop singing the same old songs of blame, and confusion. God wanted me to take this record off the player.

It seemed like taking this step would create problems for me. Every time I imagined breaking up with this person I imagined the trouble and heartache that might follow. But God was true to His word. Resisting the temptation to cling to this relationship was a moment in time that broke me free of that vicious cycle.

It might have been the first moment where I realised that in order for my life to change I didn't just need to change my boyfriend or my circle of friends. I didn't just need to change the city I lived in or the producers I was working with. I needed to look at me – **I needed to change.**

Up until this point my life had seemed like a broken record. Since I'd begun making those mistakes in my teens I'd continually made the *same* mistakes.

Becoming a Christian came as something of a shock for my family. They'd watched me as a troublesome teen and a lost young adult. They'd been there though it all. Now this 'Jesus' was happening, there was a mixture of relief because it was quite wholesome after all, as well as concern.

This was a challenging period. Living back at home and spending a lot of time with my family again, whilst attending a church full of young people regularly, and suddenly talking about nothing but Jesus, meant that tensions would rise.

As any loving family might, they began to test me on my beliefs. I had not yet begun to live out a life of faith. They were yet to see God at work in my life. My dad in particular had some concerns that all the dreams about my musical career we'd once shared were a thing of the past. The word 'brainwashed' was used to some offence, though initially the challenge came from concern. It was probably my first experience of opposition to my faith, something that I had been reading about in my New Testament.

the song...

I felt some massive differences in myself when I gave my life to Jesus. I felt instantly more aware of, and more motivated to challenge my faults. I also felt determined to live a life that was pleasing to God. But I was still operating in a mindset that had been shaped by the world. It was a world that says 'look after number one', 'do whatever makes you feel good'.

The Bible was entirely new to me. I'd read snippets of the New Testament and heard people speak at church. I was finding the teaching amazing and was soaking it up like a sponge. But it was all still so new. I was struggling with principles that I'd never really considered before.

I found myself at the beginning of a journey that as a Christian I will always be on. I was learning about denying myself, making myself less of a focus, and God more of a focus. I'm daily learning to fight against my urge to respond rashly and selfishly. The more I read of the Bible, the more it has freed me to think in a new way. It's a way that is life giving instead of destructive.

I had my first taste of this journey when I found myself shouting at my mum in some needless minor dispute.

My spirit went into turmoil as I thought, 'how can I be so selfish when I've given my life to Jesus? Why do I still find it so hard to control my temper?' It was at this point that 'New Song' began to form in my mind.

I was calling on God for help. My lack of patience was the key to my frustration with myself. The jerky time signature later used in the song was meant to highlight that impatience.

As the months passed and I moved into a house in Sheffield, began working in the City and settling into a Christian circle, my parent's views on where I was at began to change.

burning the old record...

In psalm 33 at the beginning of the chapter, the psalmist is referring to musical 'Praise'. He is literally asking us to present creative and excellent music in celebration of how awesome God is. He wants us to bring the very best of what can be created on this Earth and put it on display for His glory.

My friend Andy felt this verse had been given over his life, and the evening in the studio where we spoke about my musical future, he prayed it over me too. There's a need in our generation to produce the most exciting music and art imaginable for God's glory. I wanted to put this into a song at some point. Oddly it came to mind in the aftermath of the argument I had with mum.

Perhaps this was because I was realising that God wanted a 'new song' to narrate **my** life. I wasn't going to be under a melancholic ballad of failure any longer. I had been intended for something more than that. Jesus deserves the best of us. And He wants us to praise Him with a new life. He offers it to us freely.

He wants to see those broken records in your life, those songs of despair that are stuck on repeat, thrown into the fire and forgotten.

It says in the Bible, **'and as far as sunrise is from sunset, He has separated us from our sins'.** (Psalm 103: 12, (The Message).

He wants to remove our old songs that far away from us as well. But we have to let go of the 'old tune' that we've been singing.

I found that in my struggles as a new Christian I would often worry that I'd lost my connection with God and that I wasn't good enough.

God has forgotten our sin, and we need to let go of it too. Verse three of 'New Song' includes the Biblical declaration that nothing can separate me from the love of God that I've found through Jesus. The NIV says it like this,

'...Neither height nor depth, nor anything else in all creation, will be able to separate us from the love of God that is in Christ Jesus our Lord.' Romans 8:39

Bottom line? He's awesome, and **He deserves a new song.**

 watching me

Lord, there's something
that's been on my mind
I'm worried that I'm wasting time
Afraid I might get left behind
but I know that You're watching...

Every song I sing, every word I say to You
You know me better than I know myself
'Cos there always has been You
I know that this is true

You've been watching me
From long before I ever **dreamed a dream**
And every tear I've cried,
You have seen, You have seen
So I'll dry my eyes and look for You
'Cos I know there's nothing You can't do
Morning star, Light of the world, Jesus, Jesus

Child, I know theres something on your mind
You want to **make the best of time**
Afraid you might get left behind,
But feel that I am guiding

Every time you seek my voice,
It's my love for which you thirst
Trust in me I will provide
Learn to love and seek my kingdom first,
you are free...

Cos I've been watching you
From **long before** you ever dreamed a dream
And every tear I've cried,
You have seen, You have seen
So dry your eyes and look for me
I always have and I will always be

Your morning star, Light of the world, Jesus

I know you better than you know yourself
Trust in me above all else

watching me...

'For He chose us in Him before the creation of the world to be Holy and blameless in His sight. In love he predestined us to be adopted as His sons through Jesus Christ, in accordance with His pleasure and His will.

In Him we were also chosen, having been predestined according to the plan of Him who works out everything in conformity with the purpose of his will, in order that we who were the first to hope in Christ might be for the praise of his glory.' Eph 1:6 (NIV)

long before I dreamed a dream

At the age of twenty I 'met Jesus'. If you have some doubts at this stage, just humour me. My testimony is this, Jesus met with me spiritually, and in a moment I was changed. The next step was beginning to realise my purposes as a child of God. I had to be prepared for some huge changes. I had to lay down my dreams. My huge, intense, all consuming dreams.

Having spent so long with my eyes on music, changing my focus to 'Jesus' was a huge adjustment. I chose to surrender the plans I'd made for myself in order to accept what God may have in store. There was an exchange to be made. And as I'd long since proven that I wasn't that great in the driver's seat, I had to begin to trust in His ways. I didn't just ask Jesus **into** my life. In order to be where I was really supposed to be, I had to pray 'Jesus **take** my life'. **Let's do things Your way.**

My worst fear was that my abilities would somehow go to waste. I had it in my mind that maybe I would have to give it all up. The truth is I *did* have to give it all up, but not because God wanted to rob me. God wanted to set me free from who I was becoming and from the lies I'd believed. He wanted me **free** to be who **He** called me to be.

I had to tidy some things up in my life. There were a lot of issues I had to deal with. Firstly I had to surrender my selfish ambition. A major, and very challenging part of that was declaring that God is in charge and if he didn't want me to sing, then that would be just fine, (eek). He *is* God after all. What's more, He made the greatest sacrifice of love by giving His Son to die for me. It wasn't about serving my own purposes anymore. Life was about serving Him. The good news is that when I accepted Jesus, He came to live in me, and was beginning to change me.

The world is a difficult place to be in *with* God, but it's even more so without. You find vices to keep you going. Everything I'd once relied on to get me through the day I had to exchange for something else.

For every question I could ask God there has always has been a clear answer in the pages of this 'Bible' thing. It's funny really. I'd had that New Testament in my bottom draw for years. I'd even flicked through it a couple of times to see if it made any sense. But when I really sought God there I found Him and the answers were incredible. When you take God at His word and begin to follow the guidance, it builds your faith because you see how God works. You begin to see the evidence that His ways are better than yours. Those first few months were crucial, but God knew this and used His word to speak to me mightily, even though I knew nothing about the Bible. It seemed every time I opened it up the answers were right there.

I was worrying about what my life was going to hold as a Christian and I started to ask God about it. I was wondering whether I would ever use my musical gifts and struggled with the notion that I might get left behind.

I found tremendous peace in hearing His response.
As I started to pray and ask Him, the verse at the top of the chapter jumped out at me from my barely touched, free Bible.

'He chose us in Him before the creation of the world to be Holy and blameless in His sight. In love He predestined us to be adopted as His sons through Jesus Christ, in accordance with His pleasure and His will.'

God chose me,
He adopted me,
Philippa Hanna,
through His son Jesus
in accordance to what pleases Him what's in line with His intentions, before He even created the world!

This made me feel excited, desired and peaceful, but still unclear as to what I should be doing. What is my purpose?

Why did God choose me? To be a singer? A waitress? A missionary?

So I read a bit further through the fresh smelling pages...

'In Him we were also chosen, having been predestined according to the plan of Him who works out everything in conformity with the purpose of His will, in order that we who were the first to hope in Christ might be for the praise of His glory.'

That's a long sentence! But the gist is that God created us as a part of His plan, for His 'praise'. 'The praise of His glory'.
What is that?
What does it mean to be created for His praise?
At first I thought it meant that we were made to stand in front of Him and sing at Him. Sounds very churchy.
Knowing how awesome He is, it's not too far fetched either.

But why would God need to make a plan for that? Why would that be so relevant in this age? Obviously He knew I'd be born in 1984 and get 'saved' in the year 2004. So I focused on what the word 'praise' means and what it means to be 'created' for praise. The synonyms in the thesaurus blew my mind. We could say we'd been created to:

magnify, amplify, embroider, honour, and proclaim God's glory.

It makes sense that we could be chosen to do these things for God, especially in this age. Jesus showed me that my 'gifts' aren't what set me apart. I wasn't created for music. The gifts we are given are to make God King in that area.

A talented waiter will make God King at every table he
serves,
A talented singer can make God King of the stage,
A talented builder should honour and proclaim God's glory
in every brick he lays,
A talented businessperson will make God King in every
contract he draws up and magnify God's glory with every
handshake.

I don't know everything that God wants to do with me.
But I know He wants me to

'Seek first His Kingdom', that is to (seek Him being King)
before anything else.

To strive for Him being...
King in my heart
King in my family
King in whatever work I do
King in my love life
King in what I choose to watch and read

If you don't know Jesus He wants me to introduce you to
the King, He wants to be King of *your* heart.

Then He wants me to encourage you, to love you, and make
sure He stays your King. Likewise He wants me to submit to
you as my brother or sister in Christ; checking that God is
my King, and no one or nothing else comes above Him.
That's seeking first His Kingdom.

I've come to realise that there is a very good reason why we
should seek first God's Kingdom outside of simple
obedience. God has a plan for this creation and for our
salvation. He sees the world as we could never see it. He
sees that mankind has turned away from Him and is
defacing the Earth and neglecting to love one another as we
should. I now believe that He has planned a solution, and

we have all been crafted with special abilities to be a part of it.

Everything else in life is a happy extra. Enjoying creation, taking holidays, laughing at children playing, living a blessed life, having great friends... They will just be by-products of right living. That's the wonder of God's wisdom. It's perfect.

the song...

So I wrote the song, 'watching me' about being predestined. Since I was a child, I'd believed there was something special about my life but had always attributed that to music. Now I could see it was so much more. My life has been given as a precious **temporary** gift. It's almost like we have a brief stay in this world. We're making a journey and we've been given certain tools to see us through and help us start something that others can continue.

There was one thing I wanted to say more than anything about the song 'watching me'. I had a revelation during the first few months of knowing God and this is it;

He'd always known me. More than I know myself. More than even my mother or my best friends know me. He's seen it all! Every tear, every tantrum, every thought. And He has always, always loved me. He has never given up, even when I've been farthest away from Him.

The Lord said to me, 'You have seen correctly, for I am watching to see that my word is fulfilled.'
Jeremiah 1:12

your will be done

For the rest of my life
I will be trying to find the words
For what You mean to me
You're the giver of life always the one that I can call
And You answer me

You've given all of You
Withholding not a trace of good
And you always speak the truth
Doing everything You said You would

You're the love of my life
And You kiss my eyes so I can see
It's a small sacrifice
To surrender every part of me
And You'll never give up
'Til I'm all that I was born to be
May Your will be done in me... in me

Hope of my hope
Strength of my strength when I feel weak
I can stand with You
Writer of love You are the truth I live to seek
You make all things new

You came near to my side,
the moment that I called for You
Took me up in Your arms
Doing everything You said You'd do

May Your will be done in me
May Your will be done
May Your kingdom come

your will be done...

'Love is patient, love is kind. It does not envy, it does not boast, it is not proud.
It is not rude, it is not self-seeking, it is not easily angered, it keeps no record of wrongs.
It always protects, always trusts, always hopes, always perseveres. Love never fails'. 1 Corinthians 14:4 (NIV)

a simple love song

It sometimes seems like we're born to obsess about love. But it began to occur to me a couple of years ago that I wasn't even sure what **love** is. It certainly inspires a lot of art. We idealise it, idolise it and long for it. When it comes music we romanticise and dress it up to the nines. But we all know it's seldom so simple. Have you ever listened to the average love song and wondered, 'could love ever really be like that?'

Some of my favourite love songs contain clichés like,

'You make my life complete'
'You make me whole'
'You give me a reason to carry on'
'You are my everything.'

Have you ever said these things and meant them and found yourself wanting to take them back a few months or even weeks later? Have you ever said these things and **almost** meant them...but somehow the sentiment was tarnished by the fact that you *know* the person, and their flaws, and remember all the times when they've let you down?

It's often a little disillusioning to hear an artist giving their heart and soul to someone in a song, only to bounce back into the charts a week later with a break-up song! Whether the songs are a true reflection of what's going on in people's lives I'm not really sure. But these are the words that people are singing. These songs are the sound track to our lives.

There are arguably as many songs (if not more) about love lost, disappointment and loneliness as there are about love found, fulfilment and happiness. From experience I'd wager that the love lost songs are the more sincere.

Think Twice.
I will always Love You.
How Do I Live Without You?

Our response to being hurt seems more realistic, (however dramatic) than our response to new love.

writing love...

I wrote my first full song at the age of nine. From the first verse and chorus that I threw together, to the last vocal I wrote for a dance producer before I became a Christian, I was writing about an imagined person: a dream partner that I'd never met. I always assumed it was 'just a matter of time' before our paths crossed. I may have had a certain person in mind whilst writing each song, but there was always a need to exaggerate the reality. I wanted to believe that I had found all these dream qualities in each new love interest.
Here are the lyrics from one of the last songs I wrote before

I met Jesus

'Been looking for your love all my life
Because you make me feel, so alive
And when I'm reaching out to find my way through I just
keep finding you, finding you, finding you
There's nothing left to fear
Electrified because I got you here, by my side
I keep on reaching out, you're reaching out too,
I just keep finding you, finding you, finding you'

On reflection of lyrics such as these, I can see that I was searching for more than I could ever find in a romantic relationship. I had no reason to believe that anyone could fulfil these criteria. It's almost as though somewhere in me was a deep longing for Jesus that was surfacing in lyrics I had barely given thought to.

According to the Bible, **'eternity is written on the hearts of men'**. It's as natural for us to love Jesus and to seek Him, as it is to walk to the fridge and get out the milk. Coming to know Christ is not so much like finding a good skin cream, fitness plan or life management book, as it is meeting your biological parents for the first time. They've always been a part of you, it was only a matter of time before you felt the need to seek them and find out who you really are.

If you're like me you've been imagining a person that will fulfil your every emotional need and expectation, and who'll know you inside out whilst still loving every cell of you. You've been imagining that person from the first time you heard such a love song. If you really picture that perfect person, can you imagine that you will be equally as suitable and accomplished at the fine art of love and nurturing?

If you really think about it – are **you** 'The One'?

The truth is, if we consider the ideal partner, they are compassionate, unfailingly understanding, insightful, helpful, selfless, and perfectly in line with our life call. The burning question comes to mind.

...Does that perfect person exist?

As I listen to the average love song play-list it strikes me that our high standards set us up for great disappointment in relationships. I feel it's pretty safe to say, you will never find a person who will fulfil *all* of your needs, however close they might get. If we expect a perfect soul mate, where no effort to develop communication is required, we're in danger of searching forever. That's before we've even wondered, 'what would this perfect person want with someone as imperfect as me?'

The trouble is, if we're looking for someone to 'complete' us there will always be a hole, because nobody is perfect, and nobody will make you *or* your life perfect.

God loved me before I even loved Him. With my most repulsive attitude, in my least flattering light, He loved me before I did a dot to try and please Him or attract Him. It's amazing to think that Jesus said, **'love one another as I have loved you'**. When it comes to loving people we need to be aiming for complete selflessness as Jesus displayed. It's a very challenging thought.

I'd always been expecting a fairytale.

As I'm learning daily, both from my own experiences and the stories of others, life is just **not** easy. Love may run smoothly for a season or two, perhaps even most of the time but it is never without hiccups.
God promises joy, peace, purpose and overall fullness in life. But He never promises convenience or ease. In fact He

tells us to expect trials. The same is true of our
relationships.

What are love songs *really* about?

Whether we're telling someone that they are 'our
everything', or that they can make us 'whole again', we love
to sing out dramatic declarations of love. Looking at these
lyrics I can't help but wonder, is this idolatry? When you
give ordinary people these ideals they can't live up to, is it
misplaced worship of some sort?

I believe in romance and I believe in people. But I know that
if we expect perfection in a person or a relationship we will
be hugely frustrated. It's not that we should begin
relationships with low expectations. It's more that we
should prepare ourselves for the reality of true love by
arming ourselves with grace. Part of the preparation for
being a 'dream partner' should be to get ready for the
application of true love. Practical, considered sacrificial love
that is strong enough to cover all wrongs.

I only tend to write songs about Jesus these days. It's not
because I can't think of anything to say about romance. It's
because the things I can say to God in a song, I know I'll
never have to take back. I know they'll always be true, and
the world needs **that** kind of love song.

We are so used to soaking up a diet of exaggeration and
melodrama through our car stereos and kitchen radios. The
next generation of songwriters has been raised on clichés.
We've become saturated to the point of even allowing our
lives to imitate our radio play-lists.

The last decade has seen a return to popularity of the artist
who 'tells it like it is'. We hear a cockney songstress talking

about her boyfriend throwing up on her trainers, and we love it...because it's real. We're so accustomed to falseness, that our new wave of 'real life' artists is just a breath of fresh air.

I once wrote in a song about a teenage love...
'My soul is yours, and my heart is too - I will always be your girl.'
When you've said something like that and proved yourself so wrong, you can really begin to doubt your integrity. You'd want someone to love *you* with integrity, but you're not sure if you have any yourself.

the song

'Your Will Be Done' came out of two separate revelations. The first was that,

God's love is a love that will never fail.

The day I gave my life to Jesus the one 'true' love affair of my life began. One of the beautiful things about being embraced by unfailing love is that you can finally begin to learn how you should really love someone else. I have a perfect example of how a person should be prepared to love me before I give them my life and my body.
The second was that,

I owe God my life.

Because of this amazing love, all I want to do is give myself to fulfilling His purposes. That's why the song is called, 'Your Will Be Done'. Because I want my life to be useful and I know that if I give it to Him He won't get it wrong.

Each line of 'Your Will Be Done' is meant to be a separate, **true** statement. When you know something is true it feels so, *so* good to sing it. You feel the hairs on the back of your neck standing on end, and your voice gains octaves in range as you sing it out. There's a justice in singing a song you know is true to you.

'You're the giver of life, always the one that I can call, and You answer me'.

There is never a time when God isn't there to receive your call. And He answers. It's not like waiting for the return of the text message, or e-mail. There's no miscommunication. I'm 100% understood.

'You always speak the Truth - doing everything You said You would'.

We expect our loved ones not to let us down. Promises are very valuable, especially those made in marriage. If someone promises to love and never leave you, having faith in that promise is vital to the health of the relationship. But if they forget your birthday, if they say the wrong thing, even if by chance the unthinkable occurs and they leave, there is hope in God. We can trust in God to be everything He says He is and will fulfil all of His promises, because unlike us, He is perfect. We are asked to love one another above all else, but we will inevitably fall short. Instead of losing faith in love, we need to increase our faith in God and continually strive for the standards He has set.

'You'll never give up, till I'm all that I was born to be'.

It seems that True love is concerned with the growth of its subject. Like the book of Corinthians says,

'Love is not self-seeking'. Just as every parent knows that falling is a part of learning to walk, so God knows that my struggles will develop my character and my faith. His love means that He is interested in seeing me grow. He wants all

74

of the potential He has put in me to emerge, and no matter how much I may struggle; He will never ever give up. When it comes to His relationship with you, He simply doesn't do divorce.

Writer of Love, You are the Truth I live to seek

God is so good at love because Him and love are one and the same. In Jesus we see the perfect revelation of this love.

'This is how we know what love is: Jesus Christ laid down his life for us. And we ought to lay down our lives for our brothers.' 1 John 3:16 (NIV)

If we follow the example of Jesus we see that **true** love, is laying down your life for someone, considering at every turn how you might choose righteous love over your immediate impulses.

You came near to my side - the moment that I called for You

As I said in my chapter on the song 'Father', God turned up the moment I asked Him into my life. See the thing is, God had never been far from me, even though I may have been far from Him. Connecting with Him doesn't have to be a big ceremonious occasion. It's not like being initiated into a cult. It's as simple as saying, 'God, show me that You are. Please reveal the Truth about who and why I am. Please forgive me and restore what I've either thrown or had taken away.' Soon after approaching God with words like these I knew that something had been lifted.

You took me up in your arms - doing everything you said you'd do.

God can only speak the truth. Just as He conceptualised love, He likewise invented the promise. He's true to His every word. **Yes, there is a safe place to put your trust.**

As the inventor of romance He loves and blesses marriage. In the book, Song of Songs God displays passionately how a man and woman should desire and honour each other. It's pretty amazing! There is probably no greater blessing in the world than to partner with someone and become one flesh inside God's love and promises. But even with those promises in place, people can hurt and disappoint us. We can rely on God to never change. He will never love us less; never go through a change of heart or a mid-life crisis. God will never cheat on you. God loves you for deeper reasons that you can imagine, and nothing about life will affect it. He'll never give up on you.

The final truth that I love to speak through this song is that I have a purpose in God that is deeper and more enduring than romance. I was made for good works in Him according to His purposes. Like I discovered when I wrote the song 'Watching Me', I was made 'for the praise of His glory'. All the hopes I have ever pinned on relationships are put completely in perspective by this truth. To belong to Jesus is the highest honour.

'May Your will be done in me'.

I see the numbers last
and lost, growing
That desperate look inside their eyes, showing
Now all I need is a lot more than I have
But it's ok, **there must be some way**
That I could get involved

But I'm too concerned with other things, mostly
And there's too much noise **to listen in closely**
So I'll just point my finger over there
Lay the blame elsewhere
Do I really care?

Take my heart, set me free
Reach inside, make it bleed
There's more to this, more to see
More to life and more to me
Take my heart, set me free
Just reach inside and make it bleed
There's more to this, more to see
More to life and more to me

Could I **give everything** I have fully?
When I draw close will You draw closer to me?
'Cos I cannot rely upon my strength
If I am to succeed it's Your spirit I need

Take my heart, set me free
Reach inside, make it bleed
There's more to this, more to see
More to life and more to me
Take my heart, set me free
Just reach inside and make it bleed
There's more to this, more to see
More to life and more to me

Now all I need is a lot more than I have,
But it's ok.... He is the way

more...

All things have been committed to me by my Father. No
one knows the Son except the Father, and no one knows
the Father except the Son and those to whom the Son
chooses to reveal him. Come to me, all you who are weary
and burdened, and I will give you rest. Take my yoke upon
you and learn from me, for I am gentle and humble in
heart, and you will find rest for your souls. For my yoke is
easy and my burden is light."
Matthew 11:27 (NIV)

where is God in all this?

When I start a conversation with people about my faith,
often the first question they ask is, 'Where is God in all this
then?' This is often the introduction to their passion about a
certain thing. Whether it's sickness, violence or perhaps
war, conversations can become quite delicate when they
involve a hundred and one different situations in which,
people believe, a loving God should intervene. We wonder...

- 'Why doesn't God feed starving children'?

- 'Why doesn't He stop war'?

- 'Why didn't He reach down and stop that violent
  attack'?

They're difficult things to consider, but it is natural, even healthy to ask these questions. Thankfully there are some answers with God.

The Bible gives us plenty of input on the subject of suffering, from the fall of man in Genesis to the disintegration of Job's life, right the way though to the apostle Paul being beaten and chained up for telling people about Jesus. Suffering comes up as often as a theme in God's word as it does in our lives. It's not something that's swept under the rug in embarrassment. It's not something that Christians try to ignore, or at least it shouldn't be. It's certainly not something God ignores.

Looking at the Gospels I notice that when Jesus was questioned, He was always willing to respond but would often answer their questions with another question.

Was Jesus avoiding giving an answer?

Jesus was a very controversial man. He wasn't afraid to challenge other teachers and religious people.

So maybe He didn't *know* the answer to the questions?

Perhaps if He'd given a weak response you could say so. But centuries of study into Jesus' responses would suggest another explanation.

Jesus wanted to answer questions. The people just weren't asking the right ones. He knew that changing their viewpoint was key to a person reaching understanding.

Perhaps rather than asking, 'where is God in this situation'? We should be asking...

'Where are WE in this situation? What am *I* doing?'

After I'd decided to give God a go, He began to give me a

deeper compassion for people. I'd never *enjoyed* seeing pictures of starving children in third world countries but when I became a Christian my heart started to defrost. I began to feel something **more** about it. Perhaps this was the Holy Spirit at work in my life, or my change of viewpoint. Either way, looking at things through the understanding of God's story I can finally make some sense of suffering.

In Genesis we are told how God created and commissioned us to take care of His creation. When we failed to live as He intended He sent us Jesus. Jesus said,

'A new command I give you: Love one another. As I have loved you, so you must love one another. By this all men will know that you are my disciples, if you love one another'. John 13:34 (NIV)

I began to realise that if God's story was true, if He'd made us in His own likeness, loved each one of us with the whole of his heart, and instructed us to do the same, then perhaps these issues were ours to address too. Perhaps the people at the other side of the planet who have no water to drink, and those people around the corner whose families are in pieces, are connected to me.

Maybe you have asked yourself the question, 'if there is a God, why doesn't He intervene in these situations?' particularly if, as the book of Job would suggest, He's all-powerful and mighty. The very fact that you might ask this question suggests that you have a sense of justice. You have an awareness that there are certain rights a person should have. It suggests that you have expectations of life. The American constitution states that every citizen has the right to "life, liberty and the pursuit of happiness". Deep down we all want to believe in justice and in love. They're the foundations upon which our civilisation began to establish culture.

Adam's identity...

When God created Adam He gave him an incredible gift. He crafted him with a unique identity, gave him the gifts of life, liberty and joy. However, it came at a price. With free will came the responsibility to make choices and live in the results of those choices.

I can give you examples of how God's grace has spared me from certain consequences. He *is* a God of grace and of miracles. I can call to mind countless testimonies from missionaries who've seen food, money, and intervention appear in impossible ways. But He is also a God of principles and of justice. There is a price to pay for the choices we make. The conditions for life have been established just like the stars and oceans and we have to make our decisions and deal with the consequences.

If you're not sure how God could possibly be good, let's consider for a moment for the sake of argument, that the following is true.

He made the world, then He made us and the story began. In God's story, He creates man as a stunning work of art with tremendous potential and worth. As an invention we are made in the likeness of the inventor. We are creative and freethinking. We're given a powerful and boundless gift... Choice making. In our unique choice-making nature we choose to go against the instruction of our creator, disputing his wisdom and love. We create for ourselves a situation where we have to experience negative consequences. God gives us the right to reject Him.

In the same way that we come out of the womb with gifts and strengths in the DNA, certain weaknesses and illnesses already probable in our future, Adam had a given identity.

He was created in God's image to do good works. And that is what the Bible says about us too.

The Apostle Paul writes in the New Testament, **'For we are His workmanship, created in Christ Jesus unto good works, which God has before ordained that we should walk in them.'** Ephesians 2:10

In Genesis, the very story of creation, God said to Adam and Eve, the very first people:

'Be fruitful and increase in number; fill the earth and subdue it. Rule over the fish of the sea and the birds of the air and over every living creature that moves on the ground.' Genesis 2:28

God gave Adam and Eve the job of ruling over the Earth not of having the Earth rule over them. He gave them a job to do and the free will to do it as they saw fit. In the garden, Adam walked with God daily and their relationship blessed Adam. I don't doubt that on those walks God gave him guidance and help for the works for which he was created and they loved one another's company. After all they didn't have the Bible, nor did they need it.

So as God is not in the business of robbing us, He empowered us through the Holy Spirit and the guidance in His word to attend sufferers and address suffering. We can even find purpose in our suffering, becoming a comfort for others struggling in similar circumstances. He gives us the added blessing in suffering itself of our character being shaped and strengthened. Pastor Dave Gilpin says, 'There is no greater seed that we can sow than the seed of character!'

You've been though difficult things this last few years. I know this because life is not easy for anyone. It is by very nature a journey with peaks and troughs. If you're broke, it might be that. If you're rich it might be the pressures that come with that. We all have people in our lives. And people come with issues. The more people you have in your life, the more issues you're likely to encounter.

Probably in the last year alone you can recall some level of suffering to mind, whether emotional, physical, or perhaps financial.

love me or else...

Imagine you're in a relationship. You're in love and you're fully committed to a future with this wonderful person. Then imagine that every time you look at another man or woman in a lustful way, your partner appears from nowhere and puts their hands over your eyes.

You have free will. You can choose whether or not you are faithful to the one you love. You can choose whether or not you believe this message. You can choose whether or not you respond to the invitation into a relationship with God.

So imagine, you're considering giving your life to God and He reaches down and drags you to the altar. That kind of intervention would shatter your free will. It would spoil the romance. What's more, what kind of God would force that upon you? It would rob you of your identity.

This is your identity – that you are made in the image of God, given a stunning world to live in and care for, and you were given free will.

You are a choice maker.

You can drink a bottle of wine and go home with a stranger

You can leave a restaurant without paying

You can look at a picture and see what would make it more beautiful.

You can look at a broken machine and see what it needs to make it work again.

the song...

I wrote the song 'More' in response to a change of heart that God gave to me. I began to recognise that I have a role in His plan, to be His hands and feet, and his salt and light. Realising that 'where **we** are in this' is what I should start thinking about, I felt two things...

I'm overwhelmed by the world's need...
And I'm frustrated by my own lack of compassion.

In verse one of the song I'm realising my position in the world, which might be something like yours. The world is full of need. There are so many lost and broken people who are often easy to forget while we're enjoying our blessings. And to be perfectly honest, I just didn't care enough. I still don't care enough. I realised at some point that I expect far more from my God than I am prepared to do or give.

Maybe this is one of the reasons He gives us His Holy Spirit. On the day of my baptism, five months after I decided to give God a chance, my mum gave me a silver chain as a gift. It had these words engraved on it:

'Not by might nor by power, but by my Spirit,' says the

LORD Almighty.' Zechariah 4:6 (NIV)

I just can't rely on my own strength to take on the problems I face.

burden free?

I remember watching Comic Relief with my mum as a child. We watched it most years. It's great live entertainment and we enjoy the notion that people can break the piggy bank on this occasion and really make a difference. Celebrities contribute, dress up and make us laugh and we give a few pounds for the privilege.

We enjoy the show so much that it comes as a sort of shock when the real life footage begins. When we see the comedians walking around the orphanage we begin to feel uneasy. *'This is wrong. How can all that be happening when I'm here, clothed, fed and safe'.* Then my dad comes in, takes his coat off, tired from a day's hard work and suddenly I can't really hear the TV anymore. It's taken a back seat in a matter of seconds. I'm so far removed from the reality of what's going on in the world.

In the past I've been described as a worrier. I've given so much weight to worry in my life that it's held me back at times. This is not God's will. In fact He expressly says in His word *not* to worry - that it wont change things for the better. He says if we *do* worry, we should pray. Worry should be nothing more than a reminder to pray, like a sting is a reminder not to touch a nettle, or a yawn is a reminder to sleep.

But it seems that the Bible sees worry and burden as being two separate things. Worry is clearly negative, and prevents you from achieving, whereas having a burden can help you change the world.

When we give our lives to Christ we die to ourselves in
exchange for life in Him. We hand over our agenda and our
suffering, the worldly concerns that God knows to be trivial
in exchange for His burdens and His suffering.

God never intended us to be burden free.
He intended us to be filled with light and burdened afresh
with things that concern God.

**"All things have been committed to me by my Father. No
one knows the Son except the Father, and no one knows
the Father except the Son and those to whom the Son
chooses to reveal him. Come to me, all you who are weary
and burdened, and I will give you rest. Take my yoke upon
you and learn from me, for I am gentle and humble in
heart, and you will find rest for your souls. For my yoke is
easy and my burden is light."**
Matthew 11:27 (NIV)

It seems that Jesus is saying two things here. Firstly, the
sufferings in question have been committed to Him. They're
on His shoulders. He is in charge of them.
Secondly, He gives us an option to trade in our baggage
from life in the world, for a righteous solution driven
passion to see things change.

To be burdened by Truth is far better than to be burdened
by lies.

To be burdened for someone else is far better than to be
burdened for yourself.

Let your burden be light and not darkness

Not everyone is burdened by poverty and starvation. But if
you are walking with Christ you'll want to see change in the
world. If you walk with Him you'll begin to care about the
things that He cares about. You might have some kind of

complaint to make about things, be it addiction, vanity, violence, loneliness, hopelessness or brokenness. If something about the world displeases you, you have a burden.

Empowered by the Holy Spirit you'll find tremendous freedom, even spiritual 'rest' in responding to it.

In the book of Philippians it says, **'I can do all things through Christ who strengthens me.'**

When I came to know Jesus I cast all my burdens and worries upon Him and He took away my worldly anxieties. If they ever spring up to bite me it doesn't take long before His word reminds me that they are no longer mine to carry. I have to work at keeping my eyes on God's truth, and it's a daily commitment. But I now know that my worrying certainly won't change my situation for the better.

I've begun to realise that whilst I make my journey though life I have only a narrow window of opportunity to influence the world. We can do it struggling under the crushing weight of our troubles, desperately trying to offload them onto the people in our lives, or we can take off our struggles and give them to God in exchange for His righteous conviction.

The day I offloaded my troubles onto God, He took them, and replaced them with a passionate desire to communicate His hope to people. The hope that gives life and the promise of a future filled with purpose.

God has designed and shaped you even up to this moment, to make a difference on your journey. He wants you, filled with His Spirit to walk with Him and intervene in areas that grieve you. When I sing the words,

'Take my heart, set me free,
Reach inside and make it bleed,
There's more to this, more to see, more to life and more to me',

it is a reminder that I don't want my eyes on the world and to be anxious about what I wear and how I'll pay the bills. I want the freedom that comes in being who God's called me to be. I want to be more like Him. Not a worrier - but a warrior.

A worrier hides away in their safe zone while a warrior goes to the front line and makes things happen.
Worriers focus on preserving themselves whilst warriors focus on the command they've been given.
A worrier has their eyes on imminent struggle. A warrior has their eyes on certain victory.

higher

Home is not where
the broken heart is
It's not somewhere you feel you are alone
It might not be the place from which you started
But everybody needs to feel at home

'Cos home is **not a place you want to run from**
It doesn't hold you back or up or down
It's not there to remind you of what's **said and done**
Or to keep your feet upon the ground

I was so unsure
But now it seems so clear
There is a love that is so pure
And I don't have to live in fear

For He is higher
Than all the world could ever offer
and He covers all my wrongs
He is my fire, the past cannot consume me
'Cos He is where I belong

He wants to be the one I always run to
'Cos He has made His home inside of me
And I know I can't be separated
from the love of God
'Cos He gave His only Son to set me free

I was so afraid, but now I've figured it out
Any time I feel the world upon my shoulders
All I have to do is just stand up and shout

That He is higher
Than all the world could ever offer
and He covers all my wrongs
He is my fire, the past cannot consume me
'Cos He is where I belong

So I'll raise up my hands to say I love You
Forever to righteousness enslaved
Crying tears of joy to say You love me
and I am saved

higher...

"If a man loves me, he will keep my word. My Father will love him, and we will come to him, and make our home with him." John 14:23 (NIV)

where is home?

Is home the place where you live?
When was the last time you felt 'at home'?

Cast your mind back for a moment to when you last had that 'home' feeling. You may have been by your fire watching kids TV, your mum in the kitchen making tea. Maybe it was last night when you got in from work. Maybe you don't remember the last time. Maybe there's never really been a time when you've felt at home.

I'm not an expert but I do know that families are by nature, complicated. People are complicated, so putting a bunch of them together makes for many complications. Not only are there a huge combination of relationships to look after, but there are an infinite number of wrongs that need covering.

I've learned from verses in the Bible that God is a fan of marriage. One of the huge benefits of choosing not to have sex until you are married is that children are less likely to be born into broken relationships.

When parents separate under hostile terms, it can be very difficult to muster enough love for each other that things will run smoothly for the children. People are keen to move on from the hurtful memories and start new families. They want to make the best of their lives and make fresh plans. New partners come onto the scene, and to give their new relationships the best chance of survival; creating some distance is often necessary. Accommodating the needs of their former spouse isn't always first on the list.

With every family there are most likely hurt feelings, harsh words and imperfect actions that need regular forgiveness. God says that **'love covers a multitude of wrongs'** so it definitely helps to have him at the centre of a family, and there *will* be wrongs because people are complicated.

I've seen what happens when people push loved ones away, intending to cut them off forever. Sometimes there's just too much pain to deal with and our own grace is not enough. God's grace is enough. **That is a promise He makes.** We are bound to be hurt by the people we love the most but **His love guarantees there is hope for forgiveness and healing.**

Seeing people through His eyes makes them a lot easier to forgive, as you begin to view **yourself** through His eyes, seeing how **you** have been forgiven.

my many wrongs...

However 'nice' I might seem, however 'decent' a person I may have been prior to becoming a Christian, I was guilty of many wrongs, especially by the Biblical benchmark of love.

'Love is patient, love is kind. It does not envy, it does not boast, it is not proud.
It is not rude, it is not self-seeking, it is not easily angered, it keeps no record of wrongs.'
Corinthians 13:4-5

As a friend and family member, I was, (and still am) guilty of overlooking people's needs, being ungracious, self-seeking, quick to anger and quick to take offence. At one point or another, all the things God mentions above I have totally ignored in favour of myself. When people hurt my feelings my head often fills with thoughts like, 'Why shouldn't I take offence? I'm right!' These I suppose are common thoughts. It might even be deemed rational thinking by the world. But as I began to consider God's view of love my heart started to change. Looking into his word was like looking into a big mirror displaying the truth about my attitude.

Plenty of people would probably have said I was 'a nice girl'. But I had some very bad people habits and a very sketchy love ethic. In my own wisdom, and by the world's benchmark of love I was normal. But if I look at Corinthians 13 I have to admit I was quite stupid, even with my best efforts.

I love you, baby...

People need a tremendous amount of love. Everyone in your family does. You do.

It's so easy to forget, when you're busy living life, that the businessmen sipping wine and studying spreadsheets, the workmen trailing in from the site across the road, the students in vintage wear, all need a huge amount of love.

When you look at a small child it's so easy to see how much they need to be provided for. When it comes to our need for love, we're still just kids. Maybe that's why we hear so many people call each other 'baby' when they're in love and especially in songs. Being in love makes you suddenly able to see them with protective adoration.

When I first began waitressing I noticed a broad spectrum of characters traversing the restaurant on a daily basis.

Friendly locals, cement covered labourers who can't say 'thank you' enough, charismatic barristers, young professionals that look like they're playing grown-ups in their new suits, lonely regulars, couples, old friends, posh old ladies with big brooches.

My day would always be very up and down. I'd buzz from the warmth of certain customers and how they'd appreciate and acknowledge my hard work. They might even wink and leave a pound or two to say thank you. Then I'd struggle with others. If you've ever worked in retail or hospitality you'll know that the customer is *not* always right. They might even be quite hostile, particularly if you've made mistakes or appeared flustered.

For some reason, a Bible verse began to bounce to mind and something startling happened when I put it into action. God says,

'Above all, love each other deeply, because love covers over a multitude of sins. Offer hospitality to one another without grumbling.' 1 Peter 4:8

I decided to experiment with this approach, just to see if it might change things a little. I observed quickly that the response was different. I began to see that really, what each of these individuals needed was some simple TLC.
I noticed that if I addressed a complaint with *genuine*

concern; if I was willing to admit fault; if I was focused on their needs and not my 'rights' or my 'status' issues, a peace would fall over the situation. Their basic need to feel heard and validated had been met.

what would Jesus do?

In the beginning rudeness from customers would really exasperate me, mostly because I felt frustrated that they saw me as inferior. It came out of insecurity about my position in life. But looking at Jesus caused me to seriously question this attitude.

When Jesus walked the earth He was the highest royalty. Though few people realised it at the time, He was arguably the most influential man in History. But even as He was led to execution as a truly innocent man, an exemplary person, and teacher of love, peace and righteousness, He didn't assert His importance. Instead He willingly placed Himself in the undignified position of hanging on a cross, as would a criminal, for everyone who was lost, messed up, and far from knowing God.

He gave His life for people who actually *hated* Him. He didn't live life in fancy accommodation with a huge entourage and excessive finery. There wasn't any task He was unwilling to do. During His ministry, he was treated like a criminal, with torture, mocking and humiliation but He wouldn't rebel to prove His power or royalty. Not because He was shrinking back in fear, but because He was serving us. He had a task - to stand in place of us in death so that we could be reunited with God. Jesus' eyes were on God's plan and His security was in God's call. He knew who He **really** was.

You may feel some sort of separation right this moment.

There might be some distance from feeling settled in your own identity and in knowing why you exist. Jesus went through all of this so that the distance would disappear and the cloud would come away from you. We just have to look to Jesus and His act of love and begin to believe in Him. His love covered **all** of our wrongs.

Pretty soon I found myself at a stage where my day was more consistent. Seeing what Jesus had done for me stopped me wanting to prove something about what I was worth.

you're <u>not</u> a disaster

My Dad is a very kind person. When I was little, he would spend his last penny on a bag of sweets for me. My Mum is also a kind person. After I admitted the night before exams that I'd failed to revise, she raced to Meadowhall for books and videos that might help me scrape a pass. My Mum and Dad have always tried to be gracious and loving towards me.

But as a teenager and young adult I could still think of a hundred things to shout at and blame them for. Over time I developed paranoia that I might be nothing more than a disastrous mixture of hereditary character flaws. It didn't occur to me to see that I have a fascinating mixture of my parents' strengths and gifts. Aside from that, God created each of us with our own mind, our own gifts and our own identity. There comes a point where we can't blame our genetics for the struggles we have and we don't have to make the mistakes of past generations.

The past doesn't have to be your present...

I used to look at my present with past-shaped eyes. I was buying into the lie that you're somehow doomed to make the same mistakes that you see in your family history. But with your eyes on God you see that He has a unique plan for you.

You're not defined by where you begin life...

Jesus loved His mother and brothers. But when it came to the purposes of God on His life, He was up and off. The people in nearby villages said, 'Aren't you Jesus the Nazarene', the son of Joseph and so on. They tried to narrow His potential by reminding Him of His worldly identity. But although He was deeply fond of His family, and would love them dearly, He wasn't held back by the attitude that His potential ended in his hometown. Despite all appearances He held on to the promise that **there was more.** If you've been following any kind of deeply routed dream you probably have an idea of what that feels like.

Home is not where the broken heart is...

I know people who've had lies spoken over them their whole lives, even by people who are supposed to love them. They've been told they're useless and worthless. They've been told they'll never amount to anything. **People can make you feel worthless.** After a while they don't even have to say anything negative anymore because you begin to fill in the blanks yourself. But like I realised in the restaurant, being spoken down to doesn't reflect your worth. The most important person there is or will ever be- gave His life for you. God showed how much you're worth through this act of Love. As a result, you're free to come before Him in heaven and He will see you for all you do and all you are.

When it comes to your worth you only have to look at God's

sacrifice. What He has done to be in relationship with you shows you just how much you mean to Him.

the song...

In the song higher I talk about how God has made His home in me. This is what happened the moment I asked Him to enter my life and fill me with His Spirit. When we make our home in Jesus our call is to love as Jesus loved us. Jesus is your status, your identity, **your Home.**

You are the temple of His Spirit. That Holy Spirit can only love people. Even people who don't love you. If we want to make God King in these situations, the only way to do it is by love.

We only have to look at the 'King of the Jews' bleeding vulnerably on a cross to realise that abuse doesn't make you worthless. His sacrifice and humility meant that He could achieve a great victory.

We are now free to make our true home in Him and can have that home for eternity. His response to abuse was to die in place of His abusers. Can any of us say that our response would be so awesome?

It's like a violent criminal standing up to be sentenced and a former victim standing up to say, 'let me be punished in place of this man'. It's more than forgiveness it's pure grace.

The tremendous thing about writing a song inspired by a Bible verse is that it suddenly holds eternal truth. It will become relevant in different ways time and again. This song in particular has become like a declaration for me. Time and again I've found myself about to go on stage and challenged by something, perhaps, nerves or fear. Perhaps feelings of inadequacy or incompetence.

As I've begun to sing the words I've felt God speaking to my heart all over again. He's telling me, He is higher, He is bigger, and nothing can separate me from His love.

thirsty

If you only knew how
beautiful you are
You wouldn't be questioning how
loved you are
If you had a clue **how much** your life was worth
Even in suffering you'd know it's worth going through

You like to talk about it, so lets talk **some more**
Deal with it while it's in your mind
Your heart is **opening** but you're just not sure
So many answers left to find

Don't stop, go a little deeper than you dare
Walk out, on the water you'll be ok there
Don't be afraid of the wind and waves
You're not lost alone at sea
But I know you're thirsty

Now you've got some truly beautiful ideas
And you're open to truth in everything you hear
But your **heart is adrift** just waiting to wash in
'Cos you're tired of losing
when you know you were born to win

You know you're **close to something**
You're breathing in
The cleanest air you'll ever breathe
There's **nothing safer** that you
could put your trust in
There's no other truth you should believe

And this is free
It's everything you need and it is free
And you **won't be hung over Sunday** this is free
It's everything you need and it is free

thirsty...

"Jesus answered, "Everyone who drinks this water will be thirsty again, but whoever drinks the water I give him will never thirst. Indeed, the water I give him will become in him a spring of water welling up to eternal life." John 4:13-15

sharing my free drink

It seems natural to think of your best friend as a brother or sister. As a little girl I always used to pretend my playmates were my siblings. We even used to fib about it to the new kids at school - (though I'm sure no one was fooled).

Becoming a Christian has an incredible dimension to it of becoming a part of God's family. It's incredible! Meeting all these exciting people and knowing we are one family reminds me of that childhood ideal.

Soon after to my decision to follow Jesus, I began to learn what it was like to desperately want someone for God's family. Looking at a person through God's eyes, seeing their gifts, and dreaming of all they might become made me giddy! I could imagine the exciting things God might do with my new friend's talent if only He could get his hands on it!

If you're not a believer, you might be bewildered as to why Christians seem so eager to share the Gospel with you. There are many reasons, including as I mentioned before, that your potential to impact the world is so exciting.

I've often wondered since becoming a Christian, 'can I ever really talk someone into believing this?'

If you are an atheist you'll probably say, no.
If you're not sure about faith you might say, maybe.
If you're a Christian you should probably side with the atheists and say, no. If you could argue your way into someone's heart there'd be no singletons!

broken heart, open heart...

I wrote the song 'Thirsty' from a response my heart was making to this new friend. As I looked at him it struck me.

This person is living a life. He's consumed in it and it's playing out around Him like a story. But the story is not going the way he would like.

The more I got to know this new friend and learn about his life - the more I was seeing areas where God's love would bring healing and restoration. It was like watching myself before I knew God.

There is a moment closely before I came to faith that sticks in my mind. I'm lying in the bath, surrounded by candles and relaxation music, in an effort to find some peace. The thought that kept resounding in my head was, *'this is not my life. I feel like I should be somewhere else.'*
I felt like I'd somehow strayed from the right field and couldn't make anything I planted grow.
Now, with this sense of fulfilment and purpose I felt so excited at what God must have planned for all the people in

my life who were yet to know about Him.

flowers in pots...

I moved to Sheffield shortly after finding faith and made friends with a youth pastor named Andy Rushworth. Andy is anything but the picture of a typical minister. With his faith literally tattooed over most of him and his demeanour more 'punk' than pastor it's not surprising that young people flock to hear his passionate unapologetic teaching about Jesus.

Andy loved to use war films to illustrate his points about God but on one of his milder Sundays I remember him using an illustration of flowers. He said that each of us should be like a stunning, sweet-smelling flower that stands out and brings pleasure. In a nutshell, **our lives should be worth putting on display.**

I've noticed that when ordinary people give their lives into the right hands to be shaped and formed, they can become utterly amazing. I found this illustration in the Bible.

There's a passage in the book of Corinthians where we can read about a treasure that's kept in a jar of clay. This is odd, as usually we would keep our valuables in a vault or safe. A clay vessel is pretty easy to crack into. Upon inspection this 'jar of clay' the passage refers to is chipped and cracked. It's not even a special jar; it's just an ordinary pot.

The writer is referring to us. We're just ordinary vessels with the capacity to be filled with extraordinary treasure.

Andy Rushworth was the leader of an intriguing youth group in Sheffield and I was eager to get involved with his

thirsty

vision. I came across some astounding young people. At first I figured they were a just a privileged lot with good breeding. Whilst that may have been somewhat true, I found more and more that *God* was making them outstanding. They had vision, passion and motivation for life like I'd never seen before.

Our lives are like flowers that grow from the treasure of God's Holy Spirit.

When I asked, 'Jesus, take my life and please do a better job than I'm doing!' my desire was that God would take the pot I'd managed to misshape, and remould me into something useable, a holder for His treasure.

My desire is that something beautiful, something worth putting on display will grow out of the treasure God has put in me.

Stained glass is a beautiful creation in itself, though it's nothing without light streaming through it. It reminds me that although we've been well made, our beauty becomes stunning with the light of Jesus. It made me reconsider the potential we have as individuals.

A person could go from being a creative team member in the workplace to being a pioneer in their generation.

They could go from being an entertainer to changing the way the world is entertained.

From being the life and soul of the party, to using charisma and wit to share a life giving message to the youth of the nation.

I began trying to dream for my friends as God might dream for them. As I started to see that God takes ordinary people and does extraordinary things with them, suddenly nobody seemed ordinary anymore. The possibilities were endless.

As I mentioned in my chapter about Father, a cactus can survive without water (for a time) but will it ever grow?

Think for a moment about the last frivolous thing you did. It might have been buying some shoes on eBay or perhaps it was the cocktail-a-thon you had last weekend.

Is it possible that there's something vital you've been doing without for a while now?

When I was a child I'd have a strange feeling from time to time. I termed it the 'thirsty homesick feeling'. It was an odd feeling that there was something I wanted but I didn't know what. I've spoken to several people since that were filled with glee in recognition of that same feeling.

Was it a drink? Was it a hug? A nap? A sandwich?
I wanted to cry because there was something I was craving for that I couldn't place.

You need the living water to live

Even now I have an odd habit of opening the fridge door just to see if there's anything in there I want. When I come in from travelling and working the first thing I do is switch on the kettle. When I first sit down I reach for my laptop to check my inbox.

Not all of these things are bad. Sometimes you might benefit from checking your e-mails or opening the fridge for a snack. But I have often wondered why I'm such a consumer.

Why does one drink always lead to two?
Why am I planning my lunch during breakfast?
Why am I such a fidget?

The passage of scripture that opens this chapter contains words spoken by Jesus. He struck up a conversation with a lady who had stopped by a well to get some water in the middle of the day. The lady was **thirsty.** As He spoke with her about her life, her needs, and her thirst. He pointed out,

"Everyone who drinks this water will be thirsty again, but whoever drinks the water I give him will never thirst. Indeed, the water I give him will become in him a spring of water welling up to eternal life."

Jesus wasn't saying that drinking water was always bad. He was looking at her life, and seeing that she was in desperate need of refreshment. When he spoke of living water He was actually addressing the true needs that were driving this lady's lifestyle. Without being told, Jesus knew that this Samaritan lady had been married five times and was living with a sixth man that was not her husband. We can only speculate as to why her past had gone this way. But Jesus seemed to be aware that her problem was rooted in thirst. **She was in need of something deeper and was searching in the wrong places. No relationship could fill that void in her life.**

He offered her the ultimate solution to her constant need to fill that void. God talks in Isaiah about the gift being 'free'.

'come, all you who are thirsty, come to the waters; and you who have no money come, buy and eat!' Isaiah 55:1

I think this is key to our understanding of God's offer as well. The good gift of living water is **free**.

Any other source of refreshment in life will come at a price. In the case of the Samaritan woman the costly source of fulfilment was relationship after relationship after relationship.

It might be worth mentioning at this point, that I hadn't read these Scriptures at the time of writing the song. I may have heard references in sermons etc. but as I began to form these ideas I didn't directly consult the Bible. This is one of many instances since my journey with Jesus began, where ideas have come into my heart that the Scriptures have confirmed. It's not my message, my argument, or my desire. The Word has come to life in me. And this is God's desire. He wants my friends for his family more than I could ever do.

There were two things about my new friend that suggested thirst to me. There was a natural openness to ask questions and seek answers, almost like a thirst in his character. People can be described as having 'a thirst for knowledge'. You can usually recognise these people by how full of ideas and theories they are. They soak things up like a sponge.

Secondly it seemed he was always trying escape or distract himself from reality. Whilst thankfully it was only a phase, it reminded me of many other scenarios I'd been in and seen my friends go through.

We seem to develop unhealthy habits when we're feeling empty, like the Samaritan woman at the well, going from man to man. She stopped to get some water and Jesus picked up on her real thirst. Right then and there He offered her the alternative she needed.

The hangover, the embarrassment, the bank balance, the wasted day spent recovering in front of the TV whilst trying to force down a full breakfast. Why are we always thirsty? When I read the Scripture of 'the woman at the well', it made so much sense. There is a drink that won't leave you dry and hung-over. It won't leave you confused and in need of another distraction.

The living water that Jesus gives you... **is free.**

the song...

My song, 'Thirsty' was meant to share God's heart with my friend. I wanted him to know how much he is worth, how much he needs Jesus and how empty life's 'fixes' really are. Everything we drink from this world is costly and it runs dry.

A bottle of wine might keep you going tonight, but it will run out tomorrow.

Casual sex and one-night-stands might bring some fun and distraction, but complications and loneliness so often arise.

If I look at my past it's easy for me to see that I was searching for something to fill the emptiness. After I gave my life to Jesus something happened in me. Suddenly I became complete. I felt whole. I finally could see enough value in my life to control my reckless behaviour. This is another reason why I'm so eager to let people know about the love of God.

Going back to my experience in the church meeting, afraid of what was going on around me and nervous about being the only person there who wasn't a Christian, I came to a crossroads. I'd been faced with the same questions numerous times but at that moment I decided to go one step further than I'd done before.

What I wanted to say in 'Thirsty' was this,
If you're thirsty, look into something that'll fulfil you for the rest of your life and into eternity, not just for this moment.

God is bigger than the trials that will face you when you give your life to Him. Whatever it is that stands in the way of your faith – God can lift you over it. Perhaps, just as it had for me, an opportunity has arisen for you to **go a little deeper than you dare.**

love divine

I'll say what I can
though there are **no words**
Believing in silence your tears will be heard
The **things that go on** defy explanation
The same hand that does you wrong
pleads for salvation

Though it seems all is lost,
in time **you can heal**
Though I can't pretend to know how you feel
You may be afraid but you're never alone
Look to the light to lead you **back home**

If you **just** trust
in love divine
I know you'll find the **strength** inside
When you're down on your knees, Like you've
come **to the end of the line**, Start it today,
remember the way is
love divine

Sometimes it can seem, life knows know charity
But if you look closer it's easy to see

Though you can't understand the actions of man
Start with yourself show him grace if you can

If you just trust
in love divine
I know you'll find the strength inside
When you're down on your knees, Like you've
come to the end of the line, Start it today,
remember the way is
love divine

love divine...

'But I tell you who hear me: love your enemies, do good to those who hate you, bless those who curse you, pray for those who mistreat you.' Luke 6:27 - (Jesus)

trusting in love

At a time when I was very new to Christianity, a hugely challenging situation came up. I'd quite randomly become friends with a person whose family life story was difficult to get my head around. He and his brothers had a rotten home life as kids, with 'dads' coming and going and leaving a wake of abuse. Children in the family had grown up using drugs, violence, and crime to take the edge off reality. A few years ago one of the brothers in the family was lost to suicide leaving the remaining family in further desperation and darkness. It was a kind of wake up call.

It just seemed like a bad dream. After everything the family had been through it wasn't even that much of a shock. It had been dreaded and foreseen for some time. Perhaps that's what makes it so unbearable. Watching your fears for someone in a desperate situation become a reality.

I found myself wanting to offer some kind of comfort. I quickly realised however, there's nothing very helpful to say to someone whose brother has just taken his own life. Everything you say sounds detached and flippant. It's difficult to point your mind to the joyful years that have preceded this terrible event. It seems pointless to ask, 'how are you coping?' There's an almost visible cloud over everyone that says - 'this shouldn't have happened. We shouldn't be saying goodbye. Couldn't we have done something to change this?'

There's only one solution to the senselessness of a whole family that's draped in this kind of darkness. There's a real need for a complete turn around in thinking and being. There's a need for deep healing and a change in direction.

Addiction is such a powerful snare. So many addicts try to get clean. According to government surveys the average 'stay clean' rate for rehab candidates in the UK is about 13-14%. Those kinds of figures inspire little hope for addicts and their families. So why the grim outlook? A number of factors have helped produce this number. Once the initial detox is complete, a long slow process of healing has to begin. Part of this may include revisiting experiences responsible for the initial uptake of substance abuse. This can be painful.

On top of that, there's the lifestyle to kick. We're all creatures of habit. Most of us have comforts that we lean on, anything from tea, to TV. For those struggling with drugs and alcohol, it's even more difficult for them to escape their daily patterns, the circle of friends, and the daily visits to certain places. Just when they think they have done it, an old face will turn up at the door. The temptation is fierce. It's obvious that there's a need for fundamental transformation, something powerful enough to rewire their entire operating system.

I was astounded to speak to representatives of 'Gilead' a UK based Christian life-training centre specialising in the rehabilitation of alcohol and drug addicts. Gilead has an incredible 50% 'stay clean' rate at present. This is such a contrast to the national 13-14% average, that experts in the field can't fathom their secret. Gilead maintains that there is no secret at all. The simple fact is that getting to know God is for many addiction sufferers the only hope for that 'fundamental transformation'.

The need to be 'rewired' is not exclusive for rehab candidates. As a young adult my teenage years left me feeling like a person with issues. Over the past few years I've heard countless testimonies by people who considered themselves lost causes for all kinds of reasons. They had tried everything to change habits and vicious cycles in their lives. But they found just as I did that one thing could go deeper that anything else to truly transform the situation.

Getting to know Jesus.

God challenges us in the Bible to simply taste and see that He is good. If we try asking Him in, if we seek, we can find that He makes sense and He creates miraculous change.

Knowing people who've cared for addicts I've realised there is nothing a person can do to cure them. Advice, encouragement, support, even love can bounce off the surface of the lifestyle they're wearing. The problem is, we can't go down as deep as those underlying wounds and they just keep coming up like damp resurfaces after the house is redecorated. Someone needs to go down to the foundations and fix the problem. Jesus is able to do that. From His point of view, nobody is beyond repair. They can be delivered from that powerful hold in as little as an instant.

In the Bible, Jesus brought instant healing to people who

had been cast out by society and were unable to function normally. What highlights the awesome truth in those accounts is that He is still able to perform such healing today. I've shaken hands with a man who after prayer came out of a coma, instantly healed of organ failure from years of drug abuse. He was instantly healed of addiction, shame and hopelessness. He has become an example to all who hear his story. What I've discovered is that to God, to heal a dying drug addict is no harder than giving a twenty-year-old woman new life. In Him, full healing is available for any spiritual or emotional wound, and not just the kind of healing that allows you a normal life. God gives a healing that allows you to be who you were always meant to be.

If there's one time when people are most likely to reach out to God it's in grief. Perhaps this is why we do funerals at church. We even pray and sing hymns. It might be the one time in our lives where we're desperate enough to do so. You could argue that we 'created' God for this reason. But my firm belief, based on historical evidence, the fantastic power of Biblical scripture and on my own experience is that God created *us* with a deep need for Him. We can ignore this need for years, until we're pushed to the limits that bereavement brings. It seems that deep down, many of us believe that when we lose someone, all we can really do is ask God to take care of things.

forgiveness...

When bad things happen, there's usually someone we can assign blame to. In cases of abuse or negligence, to forgive the person responsible seems humanly impossible. It just seems so hard to come to terms with the idea that people can do such things. It hardens our hearts and stops us trusting those close to us.
I read somewhere that not forgiving can actually present us with the symptoms of an illness; for example, things like

sleeplessness, stress, headaches, and a general feeling of ill health. I started to notice as I was learning about Christianity that carrying the weight of unforgiveness was destructive to new relationships and to my self-image. A key part in being released from this was the realisation that *I* had been forgiven of so much. When I looked into my own life, I saw what God had let go of and began to realise that holding judgement in my heart over people who have hurt me, is massively ungrateful of His grace.

Jesus talks about this in the book of Matthew. Peter comes to Jesus and asks, 'how many times should I forgive people? And Jesus says, **'not just seven times, but forgive my brother seventy times seven times'**.

He goes on to tell the story of a servant who is in some serious debt, to the point of nearly losing everything. When he's asked to pay up, the servant drops to his knees and begs, 'Lord, have patience with me, and I will pay you'. Amazingly the master feels sorry for him, shows great compassion and cancels the debt.

The same servant then goes out to find a fellow servant who owes him money (perhaps he was looking for someone to blame). He takes him by the throat and demands payment. His fellow servant falls at his feet, and says those familiar words "Please have patience with me and I'll pay up'.

The servant refused to be lenient and had the man thrown in prison. Those nearby felt bad about what they'd seen so reported it all to the master. The master called in his servant and took him to task on what had happened. He was angry having taken such compassion on him, only for him to be unmerciful to a fellow servant. Jesus goes on to say how the servant was punished until he was able to pay his debt.

What Jesus is reminding us here is that when we accept Him into our lives, our slate is wiped clean and our debt is cancelled. The things we've done wrong against other people, God, and ourselves have been forgiven. As we're in this position we can't afford to hold people's mistakes against them, even if they are in the wrong. It's just not our job or our right. The servant was in a great position- he'd had his debt cancelled! And he was free to go about his life with a fresh start. But he let his mind get the better of him and began to boil with blame. His response caused him to go from being in a privileged position, to being worse off than when he started, as well as hurting people around him in the process.

Even in matters where we have been wronged, Jesus reminds us that we have to look inwardly before we look outwardly.

difficult people...

When I first began attending a local church, our radical youth Pastor wanted to train us in serving the church by entrusting an entire event into our hands. He initiated a programme, where over seven weeks, Christians who were mature in faith were invited to share stories with us about lessons they'd learned though their walk with God.

One week, a man of mature years stood at the front of our church meeting place and addressed us warmly.

'Life is full of difficult people, isn't it?' He began, a murmur of recognition spreading though the congregation.
He continued, *'and you're one of them, do you know that?'*
A slight glow of embarrassment lit the room full of faces.
I'm 'one of them'. It resounded in my mind.

It was such a revelation to me. I was sitting in that meeting,

ready to recall each person in my life that had disappointed or irritated me, and I was failing to see my part in that. The penny began to drop that the world is made up of difficult people that are in fact... All of us.
The world is full of cruel people that are in fact...us.
People are disappointing...We're all disappointing.

He went on to say that one of his life's biggest lessons had been learning not to be a 'difficult person'.

If there's one thing you have a shot at controlling in any given circumstance whether difficult or blessed, it's your response. Here's where our free will is given its toughest workout... When choosing our response to suffering, trial and even blessing.

A lot of our bitterness is brought about by our experiences of 'people'. Chatting over a cup of tea with a friend, the conversation often comes back to your most recent gripe with someone.

The question is- are our lives filled with people who are in the wrong? Or are we in fact surrounded by people who are just like us?

How relieving that God has appointed a person for you to put to great use. There's one person, one person that He's given to you. With His help you'll be able to put this person where they should be. To use their life and their resources to serve the ultimate vision for good.

You can decide how they respond to challenge and you can teach them anything. You can give them over to God and He will make them just the way they should be.
There's only one person, but that's better than none.
That person is reading these words.

the song...

Love divine was written as an offering of comfort for someone who was suffering. I particularly wanted to address the difficult issue of suffering at the hands of others.

At some point you may have asked questions like,
How can people be so cruel?
Why do things like this keep happening in my life?
How can I turn things around from this hopeless point?

When I wrote this song I wanted to communicate the awesome truth, that the power of God's love brings healing and restoration.

We can't always understand what makes people do bad things. But we can always rely on God to judge things fairly and to offer us full healing from what might seem like an endless cycle of suffering.

We have to stop struggling against other people. We have to stop wasting our time pointing the finger and destroying ourselves with anger and unforgiveness. It's God's job to deal with such things and He's eager to set you free from the weight of it.

He came across plenty of cruel people. His response is the one we need to follow. His response to **cruelty** was **love.** It's the polar opposite to what seems at first to make sense, yet we know that where all else fails an act of love can bring relief in the worst of circumstances.

I was once restricted to a life behind the window of a single viewpoint. Now I have the freedom to see through God's perspective and understand. To see something of the bigger picture in that desperate situation, and I can see that

I have an important choice to make. **To be a part of the problem, or to take my place in the solution.**

moonlight

No longer all alone
at midnight, The Son is **now my star**
No longer lonesome in the moonlight
You're here by my side I will **always be Yours**

Just like You said my mouth is **filled with praise,**
Heaven's song upon my soul,
Your presence here so peaceful
that I know it's true,
My whole life becomes complete
inside a moment spent with You

Alive Your grace, I see Your face,
Your holiness like summer to **my soul,**
Nothing could ever come between us now
Your perfect love has healed me
I am whole,

No longer **lonesome** in the moonlight
All alone at midnight,

Holy, Praise You on high, who died, to give us life,
Praise You, Praise You on high,
who died to give us life,

No longer all alone
at midnight, The Son is **now my star,**
No longer lonesome in the moonlight
You're here by my side
No longer all alone
at midnight, the Son is **now my star,**
No longer lonesome in the moonlight,
You are by my side

moonlight...

**'My mouth is filled with your praise,
declaring your splendour all day long.'** Psalm 71:8 (NIV)

He knows where you are

Picture a teenager you know. Maybe your son or daughter, your niece or the next-door neighbour's rowdy kids, maybe it's even you.

There's usually a sense within a group of teenagers that some degree of separation from their parents has begun. Suddenly they shut people out. Then you begin to wonder,

What happens in the secret alone times?
When the friends have all disappeared home,
When school is done for the day and all they want is to be out of the house?
Why don't they want to sit at the dinner table or go on holiday with the family?

What do they think? How do they feel? What's going on in their hearts?

Whilst I was causing havoc with my group of teenage friends,
arguing with my parents,
having boy trouble,
struggling with my body image,

dreaming of better days,
thinking about a more obedient, rebellion-free life I may
have long left behind,

I found a little safe zone in my room. Here is where my
habit of 'late nights' took hold, in the security of that alone
time.

This began following a specific period of time where I never
wanted to be alone. I would break any rule for the sake of
being with my friends. They seemed to be my therapy –
struggling with the same kind of issues. Ultimately I just
didn't like to be alone with my thoughts.

It even got to the stage where the authorities were sending
threatening letters to my parents to get me back into
school. On top of feeling stressed, putting my parents
through this heartache made life all the harder.

You may be thinking 'what parents would allow this?' My
response in their defence would be that I didn't give them
any choice. I would manipulate and hide things from them.
The worse I felt about myself, the less I was allowing them
to be close to me.

They never wanted to push me away altogether so I pushed
their boundaries as far as they would go. They did all they
could to encourage me and support me into finding things
easier. But the truth was – I was having real trouble finding
out who I was, what life was all about, whether I had a
reason to be a part of it and whether the world had any
hope in it at all. And even though I relied so much on my
friends for support I don't know if I ever even opened up to
them.

'I've been where you are'

As a teenager you may have heard these words. As a parent you may have said them. **But the truth is no one has ever been *exactly* where you are.**

The world has never been so confusing. You have the 'Freedom' to choose your sexuality your beliefs, the subjects you study and almost any career path. We have all this freedom, yet lack of direction has never been such an issue among students and young people. Your parents have never been where you are. Your teachers have never been there either. There may be nobody who truly understands what you're going though. **That is, no one except Jesus.**

After things began to get out of control with my friends, I found myself in that time old teenage position, 'grounded'. This was my worst-case scenario. All I could think was that they had no idea of the damage this incarceration was doing to me. It caused me to be alone which was my worst fear. But something happened as I retreated to my little blue bedroom. I'm sure, looking back now, that God was very near at this time.

As I spent that evening at home, rearranging my bedroom, I began to feel a peace settle over me. This room became my safe-zone and suddenly my own company became very therapeutic. I took to sitting on my window ledge and staring wistfully into the sky. I felt a presence there in my aloneness. I felt a certain sense of isolation from the rest of humanity, wondering if I really was different or special, or if there was a reason God had given me a few special dreams: I wondered if anyone would hear my voice or if I'd ever have something to say that was worth hearing. I felt that in that space I was being fed ideas about my future. Unfortunately this didn't do much to remedy my nocturnal nature. But the stillness of the night gave me so much space to dream and fantasise about the fulfilment I was seeking.

One of biggest problems during my teenage 'crazy days' phase was that staying up all night usually meant sleeping most of the day.

The night became a place of thinking and peace and restfulness for me. But it was a false rest. Because the next day I'd have to pay the price in not being able to get up for school, or not being able to face lessons. As I left school it was still a hard habit to shake.

the song...

My twenty-first birthday was my first as a Christian. It was the first birthday I'd had in years where I was looking ahead to a future filled with hope and purpose. My parents blessed me with a shiny new laptop to make music on. During a late night 'figuring out software' session I began to record a little guitar idea.

I was playing extra gently so as not to wake my Dad in the next room, and when I began to sing a spontaneous line or two to get a mic level in a similar softness, I felt a song rising up inside me from God. Here I was, late at night. Just me and the moon and stars at the window. But I wasn't alone. Jesus was now the hope and freedom that the night sky had once given me. So I found myself getting really into it. I ended up in a time of musical worship, all by myself.

As I sung the lines all I wanted to do was add layers of vocal harmony to it. I wanted to form a heavenly sound that would drift up to heaven and reach the angels, praising Him for making me whole. I wrote the verse and chorus to 'Moonlight' in one take and spent the following hour adding layers of other vocals. In the morning I listened and thought of it to be a nicely captured music experience. It remained hidden on my hard drive until a housemate borrowed my laptop to record something of his own. They played the song to my other housemates who all seemed to like it. They encouraged me to use it on the album I'd begun to make.

The central truth of the song is this. In the noise of my life as a teenager, I was afraid to stop and see **who I was** without my friends, without the chaos. I was afraid to face myself. What I've found is that being reconnected to God in your life dissolves loneliness. And it dissolves lies. You'll never be alone, and you don't need to throw yourself into socialising every hour of your life to ensure that.

If you feel like there's something in your life that needs healing or addressing, if you feel like things are just piling up and something's about to give, don't make the mistake of avoiding yourself. God speaks to us in quietness. There's nothing to fear in making that time to listen. And there's nothing you could share with Him that will make Him love you any less.

king of kings

You are the air I breathe
You know my **every need**
Before I even start to speak, I want to worship You
In spirit and in truth
You mean more than the world to me

And I will shout Your name
And sing Your praise
For You are **worthy of the highest place**
And I will lift You high
Above all things
Lord of Lords and King of Kings

I hear You calling me
I can **hardly see,** If I go left or I go right
You whisper in my ear
And now the way is clear
You are the light, You are alive

And I will shout Your name
And sing Your praise
For You are **worthy of the highest place**
And I will lift You high
Above all things
Lord of Lords and King of Kings

Lord of Lords and King of Kings
We worship You
Lord of Lords and King of Kings
We **praise Your Holy name**

king of kings...

"Your word is a lamp to my feet and a light to my path"
Psalm 119:105.

decisions, decisions

I've made so many wrong choices. I don't think enough
attention is paid to teaching young people how to make
good ones. The basic teaching I received from the world is
that when making a choice it's best to 'follow your heart.' It
sounds like fairly good advice. But what if your heart is
confused? What if your heart is broken? What if your heart
is sick?

One of the biggest lessons I've learned as a Christian and
as an adult is that your heart is not really made for thinking
- that's what your brain is for. Your heart can be a great
tool to use during choice making, as your feelings about
something can be a good indicator of what's right. But your
brain should oversee your heart. My heart is a big gooey,
emotional, feeling blob. It doesn't think, it feels. My brain
on the other hand, can rationalise, reason, plan and
objectify. It thinks.

I can imagine that my heart is a bit like a child. It has
opinions and desires and needs. It will try to drag me where
it wants to go and dictate my movements every day. But
ultimately I have to decide what's best for it. I can see that
whilst it may want to climb a dangerous rock-face without

any training or safety harness, my sense tells me it will probably fall onto the rocks below.

Overall, if I use both my head and my heart to make choices, I'm in quite good stead. But even then disaster can occur as you fall into wrong thinking or if you're under unhelpful influences. There can be a huge difference between thinking you're right and being right. It says in Proverbs 16:2

'All a man's ways seem innocent to him, but motives are weighed by the LORD.'

I've realised that although my ideas and actions might seem right to me, they are simply not as wise or as good as God's guidance. Sometimes what you want to do and what you feel God asking you to do will be totally different. This is not an easy thing for me to admit, as I love to be right! I think we all do. But in fact, realising there is always a right answer in God's wisdom even though it may totally contradict you, is so liberating.

It seems much of becoming an adult is learning to look after yourself, which involves learning to make decisions. As you reach a certain age there is no longer anyone telling you what to eat, when to sleep, what to wear and what to study. A daily string of decisions needs making as another dimension of what you might call 'free will'.

If I break down the chapters of my life, much of what led me in the wrong direction began with a single bad decision.

Getting in that car, with that person.
Walking out of school.
Going to that party.

The most important decision in my life was choosing to accept and follow Jesus. This decision covered every bad decision I'd ever made, because He offers a completely fresh start.

Following that choice, a series of inter-linked choices had to begin. I had to make a couple of practical decisions like where to live, where to go to church and how best to use my life to make a positive difference.

I'm not sure what part of my mind or character changed when I asked Jesus in. But suddenly, my decisions were no longer so disastrous. It seemed that God was somehow guiding me though the motions step by step.

This hasn't always helped me to feel confident of my direction. Even though God seems to have been guiding me for the past few years, I have still had a feeling of being completely clueless at times. The same is true for life-long Christians I know.

During the time I was moving towards God I had made friends with Christians in three different cities.

I had great friends in Preston at an exciting new church called the Freedom Centre where I had been attending. I'd also been making friends with people in Sheffield, and visited a church there. This was when I first met the tattooed pastor Andy Rushworth. He had invited me to have lunch with him and talked about joining the church. There was also the option of moving to London with a friend.

Each of these options was a possibility. In both London and Preston, accommodation had been offered to me at a very cheap rate. There were communities for me to join and work for me to be doing. I'd always wanted to move to London. It was where almost all my recording work had been. I agonised over this for weeks and weeks.

What if I got it wrong?
What if I missed out on being used by God?
What if I wasn't serving the most needy church?

I went along to church that evening and prayed about it
whilst the band was playing. I opened my Bible at the book
of Joshua and scanned over a few verses in my usual
impatient fashion. Feeling no clearer I sat down in wait for
Andy Rushworth to begin preaching. During the sermon,
(that to my amazement was on the very verses I'd been
reading in Joshua) the following Scripture hit home.

**'And the Lord said to Joshua, "Be strong and courageous.
Do not be terrified; do not be discouraged, for the Lord
your God will be with you wherever you go."** Joshua 1:9

If you know God and are in relationship with Him, you've
probably had moments like this. When God's Truth speaks
right to your heart and it's as if someone has unearthed the
answer. The Lord your God will be with you wherever you
go.

When I told my friend Steph, she also reminded me of this
verse,
**'Whether you turn to the right or to the left, you will hear a
voice saying, "This is the road! Now follow it."**- Isaiah 30:21

Whether you turn to the left or to the right...
Those are two completely different directions. But
whichever you choose you will know that it is right.

After you've been in a relationship with God for a while, you
may begin to feel like you're just going through the
motions. You turn up at church and worship, all the while
thinking you're too tired and should be back at home
resting from a hard weeks work. It's all too easy to take
your eyes off God and focus on the things of this world.

This is when decision- making can become more difficult again. You can start to feel like you're on your own in this. But God is faithful.

When it comes to crunch time, if you make God King in your life, your decisions will be based on the right motives. You will be looking at how best to use your life and not how best to serve your own whims. Jesus says this, **'seek first God's Kingdom and his righteousness and all these things will be added to you'.** He's promising that if your eyes are on Him, He'll provide for your every need. He won't leave you out in the cold trying to make a decision alone.

I found that by praying and spending time thinking over all these verses God began to convict me of what my next step should be. I had to use my heart, my head and God's wisdom.

Something will take the highest place...

'Worship'. It's a word Christians often use. It's used in reference to giving God the highest place in our life and showing Him deep affection and love. It's a strange thing to get your head around. There are lots of words that Christians use that at one time made me feel very uncomfortable. I would be thinking, I won't 'worship' anyone!' It made me feel vulnerable. But over time I began to see how worship was a part of my life whether I liked it or not. And chances are, it's a part of yours too.

When I was first introduced to Christianity I had a hard time even saying the words 'worship' and 'servant'. I had become so conformed to the thinking of my culture, that 'serving' someone was old-fashioned and would somehow belittle you.

By the standards of this world the idea of being 'servant

hearted' even sounded a little dangerous. It sounds a bit like being 'walked all over'. In light of all the mistakes I'd made in life up to this point, I was becoming very defensive about my character. I was doing things I knew weren't right, but still wanted to believe that deep down I was a 'good girl'. We naturally want to believe that we're basically decent people. It seems a huge risk for our self-esteem to begin to doubt this.

As a teenager I'd been conditioned into the thinking that my worth was all about working on my **self**-esteem, my **self**-belief, and **self**-preservation. The modern western woman isn't encouraged to 'submit' to a man in a relationship. The idea of 'submission' can conjure negative images.

We've been taught to protect our independence at every turn. When I look at my life before I knew Jesus I see that while I may have achieved some independence from my family, I've always been dependent upon something. For all my 'breaking free', I managed to end up enslaved to something else instead. I only had to look at the cigarettes in my handbag, the debts piling up against my name and the broken relationships to see that.

We choose to be independent of authority...
But in our need for guidance we turn to other things.

Magazines
Shopping
Clubbing
Work
TV
Horoscopes
Face book
Sex

It's not that these are all fundamentally evil things. As my friend Becky Higg points out in one of her beautiful songs,

**'None of these things can make me well, though some of them may not be bad in themselves.
Not one of them can make me whole, not one of them can save my soul.'**

Sometimes it's the man or woman in our life that we end up 'worshipping'. As daft as it might sound, we begin to take security in who we are through their eyes, and how they make us feel. Perhaps this is why it hurts so much when these relationships end. We forget who we are without them.

It's not just the loss of someone who we care about and spend lots of time with, but it's the loss of the centre of our world. We don't know where to look when they're not around to focus on anymore.

Worship is giving something **'the highest place'**, the **central position** in your life. It's giving something (or someone) your heart. And as a very wise man once said to me, 'Whatever has your heart has your life'.

Before I knew God I remember saying to my friend Roo "I'm really glad you've found God, but please don't lose yourself!" I was under some impression that God would rob him of His identity. Had I known God, I would have realised

that God gave him his identity to begin with and the world
has been trying to rob him of it since day one.

the song...

King of Kings might be the most 'worship' based song on
the album, 'Watching me'. It was inspired by feeling a lack
of direction and being afraid to step out and do anything.
Having made such bad decisions in the past I was afraid to
trust my judgement. I was used to seeing my foolishness
playing out before me in the form of real life. Even now, as I
contemplate my next moves in life, I can doubt my ability to
choose well.

But this is the realisation I had through looking at God's
promises.
Jesus is worthy to be honoured and praised simply because
of who He is. He created us, and we were made to love Him.

The simple beauty of worshipping God is that putting him
at the centre ensures everything else will be where it should
be. It puts **us** where we should be. His word is a lamp to
our feet as we walk along. We may be unaware of what's
coming next but He promises to be with us wherever we
go. All the things we need will be given to us as we seek
His Kingdom first. He is faithful to see us through life. It
was never meant to be an uphill struggle where everything
goes wrong. It was always meant to be a wonderful
relationship where we listen and act on perfect guidance.

A good way to begin worshipping is by declaring who God
is and why you know you can trust Him. As you speak out
the areas in your life where you feel you are in need of a bit
more light, declare that they're in His hands.

As in the chorus of King of Kings, it's always good to make
a statement of commitment:

'I will shout **Your** name, and sing **Your** praise, for **You** are worthy of the highest place.
And I will lift **You** high above **all** things, Lord of Lords and King of Kings.'

Though it might seem difficult to trust God with your life, the moment you make the commitment to do so you can be sure that it is in His hands.

Since I began doing this daily, my world and my whole reality have changed. I don't feel as though I'm banging my head against a brick wall anymore.

the next chapter

open eyes...

Meeting Jesus opened my eyes to so many truths about my
life that I was avoiding. He made me realise that if I want to
live the life I was born to live, I have to be prepared to grow
and change. I have to be prepared to listen to and trust in
some straight talking guidance. I've been able to realise
that the world doesn't owe me anything. I've already been
given more than I deserve. Life has been given to me and I
have a responsibility to use it and live it fully.

Living by faith doesn't make for an easy life - even looking
at Jesus himself we can see this. The work that Jesus did on
Earth resulted in His public execution. In worldly terms,
that looks like a colossal failure. But the ultimate worldly
failure was transformed into the greatest of victories. After
it appeared that Jesus' teaching was in vain and that His
campaign to free people by truth and love had failed, He
was given what the Bible refers to as 'the highest' of
honours. In the world today, Jesus is considered by both
believers and many unbelievers to be the greatest moral
teacher in history.

But even more importantly, Christian belief says that
through Jesus death on the cross He took all of our shame
and failings upon His shoulders allowing us to approach
God as Father. He made it possible to have eternal life in
HIm. Not because of anything we could ever do, only

because of His loving sacrifice.

It takes a step of faith to give your life to Jesus. But it's easy to see how faith in Jesus has set me free in so many ways.

all I had to do was ask...

What you have been reading over these chapters is simply a testimony. It's a witness statement of how I've discovered that God **is** there, **is** good and how He cares for you. He makes promises that won't fail, offers healing that can be found nowhere else and wants to free you into the life you were always meant to lead.

There's nothing so extraordinary about me. There are thousands of singers and thousands of talented musicians. The thing that brings me to life every day is the passion to share with you that God is alive. There is more to life than you might feel at this moment. There is more to **you** than you could ever imagine. There is an amazing plan for your life that will begin to unfold as you invite your Creator to manage you. You have incredible gifts that can be put to great use.

Every morning that you wake there is a day awaiting you that will be like no other. Whether you go to the same place each day or travel the globe is not the issue. Every day there is timely affirmation you can offer someone that could propel them towards their destiny. Every day there is an act of service you can offer and dozens of opportunities to bless those you meet. Everything you do counts.

If *you* have more questions, ask them.

When I first made that decision to follow Christ I signed up for 'The Alpha Course'. If you're not familiar with this, it's a

148

course that Christian organisations and churches run, to answer questions on life. You attend, have a meal, watch a teaching DVD and then break off into groups for discussion. It's a great way to have your say and put forward your case. If there's anything you feel is a grey area or any bones you want to pick, you're free to do so. Nothing is taboo and the food is usually great, (though I can't be held responsible if it's not)! I'd highly recommend it to anyone, whatever stage they may be at. There's likely to be a church near to you that's running one soon.

A lot of people begin the course not knowing God, and after learning more decide to give it a shot. I chose to go as a way of learning about my decision. I found that every week something would be said during the film or within the group discussion that spookily tied in with my thoughts during the week. I can honestly say that all my questions were addressed.

There is nothing I can say to prove to you that God exists. All I can do is offer you a few snap shots of how knowing Him has changed me.

There's no catch and no hidden agenda to my story. My objective for writing this book was to share with you some real hope. Not just hope that lasts for a while, but hope that never leaves you. My biggest dream is that you will know your worth and your purpose in life. You're amazing, you were planned and in Jesus there is someone who knows you inside out and will never love you any less.

It really is as simple as opening your heart to God asking Him to forgive you for anything you may have gotten wrong so far, and to give you some sign that He is there. I believe that in doing so, you'll soon have your own passionate testimony to share.

Thank you for reading mine

Acknowledgments

I have to thank some great people for the materialization of 'MORE'...

Firstly, Andy Baker for declaring I would write a book, then sticking to his guns even after I'd laughed in his face about it,

My Mum and Dad for always encouraging me to be creative and loving me to bits,

My Jesus for giving me hope and something amazing to talk about,

My friends and acquaintances throughout this twenty-four year journey, for challenging and educating me.

For their talent, time and attention to detail whilst picking this big wad of thoughts apart, I'd like to say a huge thank you to Steph Cook, Joel Toombs, Lyssa Bode, Tamsin Kendrick, Yvonne Cana and my mum. Without you there'd be Terrible Capitalization, bad, use of commas and sentences without

Thanks to Kate Tophill for genius design work on the book's cover and innards. Kate, it's always fun to work with you.

Many thanks also to Graham Kendrick, Dave Gilpin, Pete Dawson, Tim & Kathryn Dawson, AJ, Andy Baker, Andy Rushworth, Phil and Yvonne, Kate and all the rest who frequent the Resound Media office for their continued support hard-work, input and inspiration.

For everyone who has invited me to perform in venues over the past few years, thank you for providing a stage and helping me find an audience. Some of my most exciting moments have been in those few hours with you and whosoever came through the doors.

I owe a huge thank you to everyone who invested in my first album Watching Me. You have totally come on-board with this journey. I pray that this book lets you into the story even deeper and helps to inspire your own. I can't wait to unleash the next lot of songs!

Thank you to Sheffield Christian Life Centre and all of my church family across Sheffield and the UK! I love you guys!

Finally, thank you Joel for being my daily reality check, bringing me peace in chaotic moments and making me smile. What a blessing you always are.

God bless your steps...

Philippa Hanna

Other products available from Resound Media

debut album watching me

new album available in 2009

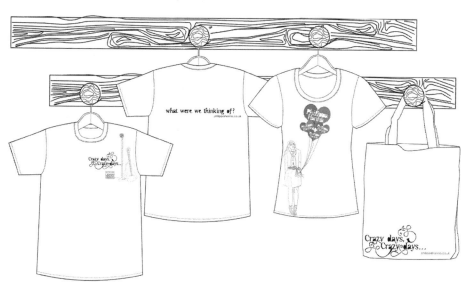

www.philippahanna.co.uk